Shaping the Coming Age
of Religious Life

SHAPING THE COMING AGE OF RELIGIOUS LIFE

Lawrence Cada, S.M. / Raymond Fitz, S.M.
Gertrude Foley, S.C. / Thomas Giardino, S.M.
Carol Lichtenberg, S.N.D. de N.

Affirmation Books
Whitinsville, Massachusetts

Published with ecclesiastical permission

Second Edition

©1979/The Seabury Press, 1985/The Marianists of Ohio, Inc.

Library of Congress Catalog Card Number: 78-25987

ISBN 0-89571-023-4 (previously 0-8164-0425-9)

Portions of this book's early chapters appeared in preliminary form in Raymond L. Fitz, S.M., and Lawrence J. Cada, S.M., "The Recovery of Religious Life," *Review for Religious* 34 (September 1975): 690-718.

Cover design by Marian Bates

Printed by Mercantile Printing Company, Worcester, Massachusetts
United States of America

Contents

Affirmation Books is an important part of the ministry of the House of Affirmation, International Therapeutic Center for Clergy and Religious, founded by Sr. Anna Polcino, S.C.M.M., M.D. Income from the sale of Affirmation books and tapes is used to provide care for priests and religious suffering from emotional unrest.

The House of Affirmation provides a threefold program of service, education, and research. Among its services are five residential therapeutic communities and two counseling centers in the United States and one residential center in England. All centers provide nonresidential counseling. The House sponsors a leadership conference each year during the first week of February and a month-long Institute of Applied Psychotheology during July. More than forty clinical staff members conduct workshops and symposiums throughout the year.

For further information, write or call the administrative offices in Boston, Massachusetts:

The House of Affirmation
22 The Fenway
Boston, Massachusetts 02215
617/266-8792

Acknowledgments

The writing of this book was itself an experience of the corporate social learning which the pages describe as necessary for revitalization. The supportive relationships that existed among the authors were augmented by a larger network of persons and communities who aided us in the total process.

First of all we gladly mention the men and women of our respective religious congregations: the Society of Mary (Marianists), the Sisters of Charity of Seton Hill, and the Sisters of Notre Dame de Namur. We dedicate this book to these our friends and companions who in everyday life nourished and stimulated our own memories and hopes.

The many religious who questioned, critiqued, and encouraged us in the workshops and seminars over the past few years richly deserve our thanks. Special appreciation must be given to Norbert Brockman, S.M., Director of the Marianist Training Network, for his continued, fraternal prodding and sage advice on a host of matters. We are grateful to the Cincinnati Province of the Society of Mary for its financial support of this project which involved several years of periodically bringing the authors together from different cities. In this regard also we are appreciative of the gracious hospitality afforded us at various times by the Benedictine Sisters of Mount St. Mary Convent and the Novitiate community of the Holy Ghost Fathers and Brothers, both of Pittsburgh, Pennsylvania.

For their patience and competence in the preparation of the manuscript we offer sincere thanks to Vera DiCola, Frank Fletcher, Dorothy Schulz, and Sue Urbanski. Our publisher warrants our gratitude for bringing this project to fruition.

Foreword

As a diocesan priest, it has been my personal privilege to be invited to lecture, live with, and exchange thoughts with men and women religious around the world. As one of the founders of the House of Affirmation, my ministry for the past fifteen years has included service to many religious and their congregations. In 1973 I had the opportunity to present a paper to the International Union of Superiors General of Men in Rome.[1]

My respect for the religious life as a special gift of the Holy Spirit to the Church has grown as I have witnessed many religious meet renewal, change, and challenge. The religious life is a special gift to all of us. The charism of the religious life encourages all Christians to more radical witness to Gospel values.

In their Decree on the Appropriate Renewal of the Religious Life, *Perfectae Caritatis,* the Fathers of Vatican II teach: "The manner of living, praying, and working should be suitably adapted to the physical and psychological conditions of today's religious . . . to the needs of the apostolate, the requirements of a given culture, [and to] the social and economic circumstances" (PC 3). The Pastoral Constitution on the Church in the Modern World, *Gaudium et Spes,* encourages us to make appropriate use "not only of theological principles, but also of the findings of the secular sciences, especially of psychology and sociology" (GS 62). The authors of this book have taken the challenge of Vatican II seriously.

Shaping the Coming Age of Religious Life is an indepth look at the current state of religious congregations in the Church. The five authors, who were all members of the Marianist Training Network, have been designing and conducting numerous workshops and renewal programs for men and women religious for over ten years. In this comprehensive book they discuss the evolution of religious life and the present period of transition and confusion experienced by many religious communities. While offering concrete decision-making techniques, the authors also stress the importance of what they call the technologies of foolishness, or creative playfulness, in the search for new and alternative futures for religious life.

This book can be a powerful tool for religious communities to recover their founding charism and discover new visions for a new time. Affirmation Books has chosen to reprint *Shaping the Coming Age of Religious Life* because its information and message are still urgent and necessary for many of us to ponder "the need to see plurality and diversity as an enrichment in the varied ministries within a congregation."[2] May this book challenge your thought and encourage your faith.

Thomas A. Kane, Ph.D., D.P.S.
Priest, Diocese of Worcester
Publisher, Affirmation Books
Boston, Massachusetts

19 March 1985
Feast of St. Joseph

---

[1] This text has been published in a volume entitled *Confirma Fratres Tuos* by Unio Superiorum Generalium, Rome, Italy, 1979, pages 22–37.

[2] Sister Anna Polcino, S.C.M.M., M.D., "Congregational Climate and Morale: The Challenge of Leadership," *Religious Congregations and Health Care Facilities: Commitment and Collaboration, Colloquium Two* (St. Louis, Missouri: Catholic Health Association, 1982).

Introduction

Memory and Hope:
A Theme

IN RETROSPECT THIS BOOK HAS TAKEN ON THE CHARACTER OF A planned happening. It emerged out of many hours of searching for understanding about the renewal of religious life and from many efforts to share this understanding with others. The progress of its writing was sometimes a sustained and focused effort; other times the project lay dormant till ideas had time to mature or criticism was able to prune away the contradictions present in initial formulations. Although many people tried to hurry the project along, it had its own pace. It would not be rushed to completion.

While it is impossible to chronicle the process of a happening (even a planned one!), it is possible once the happening slows its pace to reflect on its meaning. This introduction focuses on the origins and evolution of the book, the basic awarenesses and shared tasks which gave the book its shape, and some of the basic assumptions contained within its chapters.

The Origins and Evolution of the Book

The precise origins of this book are hard to pinpoint. The authors worked together on an informal basis for the last four or five years. During that time, they were actively engaged in the renewal efforts of their own religious communities—one as part of a General Council, others as members of chapters and commissions, and some as parts of formation and human-resource development teams. From time to time during those years, several of the authors would team together to present various renewal workshops, such as "The Founding Charism," "Planning within Religious Communities," and

1

"The Future of Religious Life." Initially, many of the ideas and models contained in this book were only partially developed. The practical experience of working at renewal within their own communities and the shared efforts to communicate the central ideas of renewal of religious life have sharpened the authors' awareness of what was important in the whole project of reanimation.

Out of early efforts to synthesize important themes, to chart the evolution of the religious-life movement within the Church, to develop some insights into the vitality patterns of individual religious communities, and to understand the processes of revitalizing those communities, a basic insight emerged that was shared by all the members of the writing team. The learnings about the meaning and history of religious life and what the authors as religious had experienced in the last ten years came together into an intriguing exploratory hypothesis: that religious life in America was undergoing a major transition, one that had been underway for at least fifteen years, and which would take another fifteen or twenty years to complete its major movements. The magnitude of this transition would be major and significant, and perhaps would be viewed in the future as one of the most significant periods in the evolution of religious life. The transition would effect a deep reorientation in the way that religious would live in community and the way they would be of service to the Church and the world. The early effort of the writing group was a search to either confirm, modify, or disregard this first exploratory hypothesis.

When beginning the exploration, three major tasks were outlined. The first was to build or investigate several models which would pose, focus, and provide insight into some of the key questions in the history of religious life and which would also provide a horizon for understanding the present upheaval experienced by religious communities.

The first of these models, which is detailed in Chapter One, aimed at providing an understanding of the historical evolution of religious life through describing the organizing concepts of a dominant image and its evolution through identifiable stages over time. This model addresses itself to the questions: Under what conditions do major innovations in religious life occur? How often have they occurred? What shape have these innovations taken? The responses to these questions reveal the dynamic role that memory plays in the contemporary search.

A second model, detailed in Chapter Two, is a sociologically oriented model that probes the life of an individual religious congregation and deals with the questions: What are the stages of vitality in a specific religious community? What are the questions and crises of each of these stages of its growing and deepening?

The third model, detailed in Chapter Three, is an interdisciplinary one articulating the possible meanings of the underlying patterns revealed in Chapters One and Two. This Vitality Curve, in exploring the basic processes of "how life is," responds to the query: What are the social meanings and the significant variables in the development and decline experienced in the collective life of the congregation and the individual lives of the members?

As work with the models "in the field" and in research/discussion sessions continued and was amplified through feedback and prayerful reflection, the conviction of the truth of the initial exploratory hypothesis grew stronger. Consequently, this reality had its effect on how the authors worked with religious communities.

The second task undertaken by the writing group resulted in Chapter Four, a pivotal chapter which reflects on the present experience of religious life. This reflection is embodied in the "transformation path" which identifies specific periods and tasks in the revitalization effort.

If religious communities are to revitalize themselves in this time of transition, then there is a need to organize an understanding of the structures and processes of community and individual transformation. Hence, the third major task highlights the hope that emerges from the possibility of creating new and alternate futures for religious congregations.

In their origins and development, religious communities

were essentially foolish when considered from the point of view of the world and most of the Church. The roots of this foolishness are essentially the nonrational experiences of a deeply religious person. The authors recognized the role of playfulness in themselves and confirmed this as significant in revitalization as technologies of foolishness were devised to aid in discovering new goals and planning for their implementation. Accordingly, Chapter Five investigates some of the major concerns for utilizing technologies of foolishness.

Chapter Six explains the approach that the authors have used successfully in formal planning and discerning. These methods of rational decision making are shown to be important complements to technologies of foolishness even while giving an appreciation of the strengths and weaknesses of rationality. The main structures of a Dialogue/Decision/ Action/Evaluation process are explained and illustrated along with guidelines for applying these processes.

It is the belief of the authors that learning and discerning out of the founding charism and its contemporary expression in the present members are central to the transformation effort. However, there seems to be much unclear thinking in this theologically underdeveloped area. In Chapter Seven the authors bring some clarity to this issue by describing the general notion of charism, presenting a methodology for recovering the community charism through the foundational texts, and raising some questions about the implications and scope of the search.

Some Assumptions of the Authors

As Chapter Six reveals in detail, the authors believe that in coming to a situation or a task it is important to surface the assumptions which are the givens that persons inevitably bring. The final section of this introduction contains the assumptions that the authors have about the revitalization of religious life. Revealed are some of the values, attitudes, beliefs, and feelings—some more unconscious than conscious perhaps—that form the foundation for the edifice to be constructed in this book. The major assumptions will be stated as themes and then briefly developed.

1. The Revitalization of Religious Life is a Faith Reality

Put simply, revitalization is a matter of sin and grace. Religious community as a human entity is an ambiguous reality. Both the reality of sinfulness in persons and communities and the reality of redemption in the graced person and community have a profound effect on renewal. The polarization of persons and the disintegration of the special bonds in community manifest sinfulness, while the wholeness and cohesion also evident reveal that grace does more abound.

An awareness that flows from the above understanding is that revitalization calls for a personal love for one's congregation and for religious life per se. The ambiguity, stress, and pain of the vitalization process can be endured only if a person has a deep personal love for religious life and for the community. In this book, the story of religious life is remembered and retold, and persons are challenged to recover the story of their community so that a deep love can be developed. But love for religious life and one's community must be realistic. This love should be based on an authentic appreciation of the community: a humble understanding of its weaknesses, and a hope for insight into its strengths which promises a newness of life.

What becomes evident from this assumption is the belief that revitalization is an intense living of the great Christian mystery: life-death-resurrection. The journey undertaken is essentially the movement of the Lord to Jerusalem.

2. The Revitalization of Religious Life Is Situated in a Cultural Context

History is only lived in the here and now. However, that the past and the promise of the future relate integrally is becoming more evident in the present crisis in religious life, which is part of a profound cultural transformation. The response to this crisis must simultaneously be a response to that transformation. The thrust of this book has been worked out in response to the North American experience of renewing religious life.

A key challenge to North American religious life is the integration of the rational and nonrational on both the personal and collective levels (see Chapter Five). This is because the fundamental and identity-shaping experiences of the religious person and the religious community are essentially at the nonrational level of human experience. Central to the project of revitalization is the need to deepen the mythical roots of one's own life and those of one's community. Revitalization means the recovery of the ability to be in touch with personal myths, how those myths brought one to a community and its unique and particular myth, and how those two stories might blend into one. Americans, immersed in a rationalistic culture, will find the challenge of integrating the rational and nonrational a particularly difficult one. This search for integration will require great poverty, and an ability to let go of what has seemed sure and true.

Another challenge which torments the culture is the demand for new approaches for integrating the individual and the community. Along with religious congregations, government, military, and educational institutions suffer from an increased awareness that all members have both a stake in and an obligation to contribute to the plans and decisions that significantly influence their lives, coupled with an inability to adequately effect these results. Fundamental innovation in this area is required.

3. The Revitalization of Religious Life
Demands Widespread Involvement

A critical distinction involved in this assumption is that between the *process* of renewal and the *programs* of renewal. The authors believe that a majority of members of a religious congregation need to be involved in the *process* of renewal and not simply in the *programs* of renewal. Hopefully the latter are a means to the former, but too often the work of "renewal teams" produces more of a rippling conformity among a few rather than the current of transformation which will draw the whole community to the depths of insight and commitment required in a crisis of the magnitude presently being experienced. Given the enormous amounts of money and energy expended in generating and attending workshops, directed retreats, community days, and the like, the image often emerges of the zealous Elijah eagerly searching for the Lord amidst the crumbling Israel. The saving Lord was neither in the heavy wind, the earthquake, nor the fire. "After the fire there was a tiny whispering sound. When he heard this, Elijah hid his face in his cloak . . ." (1 Kings 19:12–13).

The processes described in this book require strong leadership. But more than strength is needed. What needs to be released and utilized is the authority of the adult, mature human person, a quality that resides in more persons than previous stereotypes of authority admitted. Revitalization necessitates multiple roles of leadership: wisdom, prophetic, functional, and the other styles that can effect widespread participation amidst the growing diversity.

The history of religious orders reveals that congregations that have survived major transitions (see Chapters One and Two) were characterized by a deep recentering in Christ by the membership. Accordingly, the present assumption is that revitalization in the present age requires a deep personal life of faith among a *significant number* of persons in the community, not simply one segment of the congregation. This is so because religious regenesis is primarily an interior experience, even though it has significant social ramifications. Rekindling the fire of faith through prayer and contemplative listening to the Lord results in a discerning community reminiscent of Mary of Nazareth, herself faced with being central to the uncertainties of the great transition from the Old to the New Covenant.

4. *The Revitalization of Religious Life Is a Transforming and Historical Dynamic*

The commonly accepted image of religious life, as it has most recently been known, is dying. This image, which arose after the French Revolution, has prevailed among religious themselves as well as "outsiders," and afforded an appreciation of the values religious life has served in the Church and world. The assumption that this image (expressed primarily in the apostolic works of schools and hospitals) is dying means that it is no longer observed as functional even though it served the Church well.

In the process of revivification, religious congregations will recover the historical relationship between themselves and the institutional or diocesan Church. Historically, in its renascent phase, religious life plays a strong prophetic role for the entire Church. After a while the role becomes more functional though still central and positive. The recovery of the prophetic role will be an important complement in the revitalization in that it will also involve recovering the sense of the larger history of religious life. As a movement in the Church, religious life has a long, complex, and many-faceted history. The reanimation of individual religious and their communities, while always in the here and now, will be enriched by reclaiming a larger context and history than the last set of renewal programs or General Chapter.

The transforming dynamic assumed recognizes that religious life participates in the demands of all social realities. Hence, as the last four chapters of this book will describe, revitalization requires a deep transformation of religious life in its conceptual and structural dimensions. As one of the authors has put it, "We cannot be about rearranging deck chairs on the Titanic," which is how renewal efforts have sometimes appeared.

5. The Revitalization of Religious Life
   Requires Creative Social Learning

A shared framework of learning and valuing is necessary for regeneration. A central assumption of this book is that vitality must emerge out of a continuous process of dialogue. Dialogue can be successful when the participants work to build shared frameworks of learning and valuing. In the breakdown of the social bonds of religious community, the language of appreciating, that is, learning and valuing, also breaks down. The bonds are no longer capable of supporting the debate and communication necessary to sustain community. In this book, an effort is made to build a consistent language and set of models around which learning and valuing of revitalization can take place. A core activity of vitalizing a religious community is building up a shared framework of appreciation.

Creative social learning occurs at the interface of a variety of ideas, methods, and personal experiences. This book itself was the product of a social learning process which brought together people from different religious congregations, different academic competencies and points of view, and diverse styles of thinking and feeling. This approach, although difficult and at times downright painful, was extremely fruitful in enhancing understanding. The supportive collegial interaction, with its mutual criticism, testing, and revision of ideas, as well as the creative building upon each individual's efforts, enhanced the end product more than was expected at the outset.

The creativity assumed calls for an openness to the unexpectedness and the surprise of the future which includes a capacity for dreaming equal to the capacity for analysis. This will mean the ability for: *wonder* at unexpected ways God breaks into life; *dreams* to develop images of the future which are attractive and exciting; *analysis* of the present situation for understanding and insight into the impact of actions taken; *planning* with modes of community discernment which allow adventuring and exploring.

Finally, the authors have the assumption that theory informs experience in the movement toward action, and that reflection on that action helps to build new theory. The theories contained in the book are ones that have grown out of an interplay between theory and action. Ideas were generated, synthesized and structured, and communicated not only in written form but in the praxis of workshops. Then, reflection on the impact of the life of the religious communities in question served as a source of learning for further refinement, which included adding new ideas and discarding some ineffective old ones. This process confirmed the belief that one element in a successful renewal program is a vital and reciprocal relationship between theory and action.

Having revealed the origins, evolution, and assumptions of this book, all of which come out of the authors' fundamental posture of memory and hope, the imperative is to proceed to the consequences of this stance for shaping the coming age of religious life.

Chapter One

The Evolution of Religious Life:
A Historical Model

RELIGIOUS COMMUNITIES IN THE LIFE OF THE CHURCH ARE NOT
fixed and static entities. Taken together, they make up a historical process unfolding over time, and religious life can be
viewed as a significant social movement in the history of
Western civilization. In this movement, particular religious
communities arose in response to dramatic social change in
the Church and in the larger cultural and political arena of
Western civilization. They became a dynamic force in shaping and changing the Church and secular culture. They have
been both a cause and an effect of social change: the founding
of religious communities has frequently been a response to
major developments in society, and the evolution of the
Church and Western culture has been significantly influenced
by the life and work of religious communities.

One way to view the unfolding of religious life in the
Church is to look at how the image of religious life has
evolved over time and see what implications this evolution
has had for the functioning of individual religious communities.[1] The term *dominant image of religious life* is used

---

[1] Some sources used to clarify the notion of dominant image were: Fred
Polak, *The Image of the Future*, translated and abridged by Elise Boulding
(San Francisco: Jossey-Bass, 1973); *Changing Images of Man*, Policy Research
Report No. 4 (Stanford: Stanford Research Institute, Center for the Study of
Social Policy, May 1974); and Kenneth E. Boulding, *The Image: Knowledge in
Life and Society* (Ann Arbor: University of Michigan Press, 1961).

here to name a many-sided reality that includes how religious view their life and its functions within the Church and the world during a given period. The term is meant to encompass both the ideal to which religious aspire and the practical actions which embody that ideal in the everyday life of religious. The term is also meant to indicate the sense of history which permeates religious life at a given time. How do people, both the religious and members of society at large, picture the past of this way of life? What grips and inspires them about this life? Is this way of life seen as enmeshed in time or separated from passing temporal affairs? What kind of future are religious supposed to be creating, and what are they supposed to be doing to bring that future about?

The process by which the dominant image of religious life evolves in time can be characterized by a repeated sequence of identifiable phases of change:

Growth Phase. A relatively long period which starts with the emergence of a new dominant image of religious life and continues with the elaboration and development of that image. The growth phase peaks in a golden age during which the dominant image of religious life successfully unites a large number of religious communities in its area.

Decline Phase. A period of ambiguity in which the dominant image of religious life comes under questioning. Religious communities seem no longer suited to the aspirations of the age. The communities lose their sense of purpose, drift into laxity, and disintegrate.

Change-over Phase. A comparatively short period in which religious life passes through one of its major turning points in history. In the midst of a considerable amount of turmoil, variations of the dominant image of religious life crop up. Certain of these variations are fused into a new dominant image.

Growth Phase under a New Image. A period of elaboration and development under the new dominant image of religious life, which inaugurates the next great age in the history of religious life.

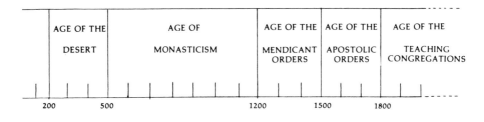

FIGURE 1.1: Ages in the History of Religious Life

The supposition that religious life has passed through a succession of such phases of growth, decline, and change-over is the basis of a model of the history of religious life that is presented in this chapter.[2] The model (see Figure 1) schematizes the history of religious life and divides it into five main eras or ages: the Age of the Desert, the Age of Monasticism, the Age of the Mendicant Orders, the Age of the Apostolic Orders, and the Age of the Teaching Congregations. Each of these ages had its dominant image of religious life, and the pattern of growth and decline described above can be detected in each age. The rest of this chapter is de-

[2] Some sources used to clarify the notion of social evolution were: Stephen Toulmin, *Human Understanding*, vol. 1 (Princeton: Princeton University Press, 1972); Anthony F. C. Wallace, "Paradigmatic Processes in Cultural Change," *American Anthropologist* 74 (1972) 467–68; Donald T. Campbell, "Variation and Selective Retention in Socio-Cultural Evolution," in H. R. Barringer, G. I. Blanksten, and R. W. Mack, eds., *Social Change in Developing Areas* (Cambridge, Mass.: Schenkman, 1965); Edgar S. Dunn, *Economic and Social Development: A Process of Social Learning* (Baltimore: Johns Hopkins University Press, 1971); and Thomas S. Kuhn, *The Structure of Scientific Revolutions* (Chicago: University of Chicago Press, 1962). The scheme of dividing the history of religious life into the five ages presented in this chapter was first suggested in germinal form by Fr. David Fleming in 1971. See David A. Fleming, S.M., "Hope-Filled Deeds and Critical Thought" (CMSM Working Paper presented to the Third Interamerican Meeting of Religious), in *Religious Life: Tomorrow*, ed. Jean Malo, S.S.S., Donum Dei Series no. 24 (Ottawa: Canadian Religious Conference, 1978), pp. 41–56.

voted to a rapid overview of the history of religious life organized according to this model.[3]

The Age of the Desert (200-500)

In its earliest manifestations, religious life did not exist as a distinct lifestyle that was lived in physical separation from the rest of the Church. Instead, consecrated virgins and widows dwelt in the midst of Christian communities during the time of the persecutions, where they led lives of edifying holiness dedicated to attaining Christ's conditions of evangelical discipleship. As the period of persecutions was winding down and the Church gradually came to be established in the Roman Empire, there emerged for the first time a clearly recognizable and distinguishable format of religious life dominated by the image of the religious as the holy ascetic. The person who came to symbolize this new ideal more than anyone else was Antony of the Desert. During his lifetime, his reputation as a holy recluse spread through his native Egypt. A year after he died, his good friend Athanasius wrote the *Life of Antony*, which contained the description of a hermit's life that crystallized the new ideal and inspired both solitary anchorites and many communities of cenobites. The desert began to take on the appearance of

---

[3] Factual and Historical data on the history of religious life were gathered from such standard sources as *The Catholic Encyclopedia* (1907), *The New Catholic Encyclopedia* (1967), the *Annuario Pontificio*, *The Official Catholic Directory*, and *The Catholic Almanac*. Some of the other sources on this topic were: Raymond Hostie, S.J., *Vie et mort des ordres religieux* (Paris: Desclée de Brouwer, 1972); David Knowles, O.S.B., *Christian Monasticism* (New York: McGraw-Hill, 1969); Humbert M. Vicaire, O.P., *The Apostolic Life* (Chicago: Priory Press, 1966); Derwas J. Chitty, *The Desert a City* (Oxford: Basil Blackwell, 1964); Owen Chadwick, *John Cassian*, 2nd ed. (Cambridge: Cambridge University Press, 1968); William Hinnebusch, O.P., "How the Dominican Order Faced Its Crises," *Review for Religious* 32 (November 1973) 1307–21; William A. Hinnebusch, O.P., *The History of the Dominican Order*, 2 vols. (New York: Alba House, 1966, 1973); Teresa Ledochowska, O.S.U., *Angela Merici and the Company of St. Ursula*, 2 vols. (Rome: Ancora, 1969); William V. Bangert, S.J., *A History of the Society of Jesus* (St. Louis: Institute of Jesuit Sources, 1972); and Adrien Dansette, *Religious History of Modern France*, 2 vols. (New York: Herder and Herder, 1961).

much more than a useless and barren wasteland. It became a place to which demons had retreated after being driven out of the cities by the triumph of the recently established Church. It was to this "desert" that generous men and women withdrew to carry on the Church's important work of doing battle with the devil in the wilderness as Christ had done long ago. In this way, the desert came to be seen as a place of austere beauty, where the monk was trained in the ways of perfection. He returned from time to time to his fellow Christians, who saw in him the power to do good—healing the sick, casting out demons, comforting the sorrowful with gentle words, encouraging the persecuted, reconciling the estranged, and above all urging everyone to put nothing in the world before the love of Christ. So compelling was this image and the kind of religious life it stood for, that the very word "desert" still evokes connotations of deep spiritual meaning to this day.

This image captured the imagination of the Christian world as news about the desert ascetics spread from Egypt to all points of the Roman Empire. The Age of the Desert had its flowering during the fourth century, as holy men and women from all strata of society were drawn to this new way of life. For the most part, the image of a solitary anchorite or hermit remained the challenging central ideal around which all of religious life focused. Some persons, such as Simon the Stylite and the other pillar saints, were given to forms of the solitary life that seem bizarre today. Others adapted the ideal to communal patterns, which resembled forms that religious life would assume in later centuries. In Egypt, for example, the first master of the common life was Pachomius. He, with the assistance of his sister Mary, founded an entire network of monastic communities for both men and women which numbered in the thousands, perhaps more than ten thousand. A bit later, Basil founded a community in Asia Minor after visiting the monks of Egypt, Palestine, and Syria. He advised his religious to always join some form of apostolic service to their community life. The chief organizer of communal asceticism in Palestine was Melania the Elder, a patrician widow of high rank in the Roman Empire who became one of the dominant figures of religious life during her lifetime. When she learned of the ascetic ideal, she journeyed to the Egyptian desert and visited the most famous hermits of Scetis and Nitria. She then went on to Jerusalem, where she founded a monastery for fifty women on the Mount of Olives. Nearby she established a second monastery for men, which she placed under the guidance of Rufinus, one of her disciples. In the year 400, she returned to Rome to seek new recruits for the monastic way. One of her arguments for religious life, which she advanced before the Roman Senate, was the danger of barbarian invasions. In her interpretation, the imminence of this danger indicated the nearness of the eschaton. For most of her life, Melania was a friend and confidant of Jerome, who visited her on his grand tours of the eastern part of the empire. However, he turned against her in her old age because she insisted on defending one of her spiritual sons, Evagrius Ponticus, who after his death was suspected of being an Origenist. Melania stands out as one of the leaders of this first great age of religious life, who in various ways was associated with many of the important persons in the movement while it was at its peak.

Evagrius Ponticus, who was the occasion of Jerome's rift with Melania, is surely one of the most colorful as well as important characters of the age. In his youth, Evagrius was a disciple of Basil and was ordained deacon by Gregory of Nazianzus while the latter was bishop of Constantinople. The brilliant eloquence of the young deacon soon made him famous, and his future seemed promising. However, in 382 Evagrius showed up at Melania's monastery on the Mount of Olives in flight from an adulterous love affair in Constantinople. Melania offered him motherly solace and advised him to become a monk in the Egyptian desert. He then left for Nitria, where he led the life of an ascetic until his death in 399.

In contrast to the more rustic ascetics, Evagrius was an intellectual and the first theoretician of the spirituality of religious life. Even though a large part of his writings were lost or remained unidentified until the present century, many of his ideas and theories became well known and still influence religious today because of an odd chain of events. Evagrius, it happened, was the teacher of John Cassian, who in turn was one of the teachers of monks of the West because his writings were required refectory reading in Benedict's Rule. In this way religious life has been for centuries indirectly exposed to the theories of Evagrius. While the Evagrian theory of religious life is basically Christian, his ideas are laced with threads of Stoic and Neoplatonic thought. He downplays the will and especially the emotions in favor of the mind. For him, the basic objective of asceticism is "apathy," a condition devoid of emotions and bodily reactions, which permits the mind to cleave to God inseparably in contemplative union without distraction from the body or the active life. Jerome was not the last person to question Evagrian thinking. Even today some commentators wonder whether or not notions such as those described had a harmful effect on the development of religious life.

The main events of the Age of the Desert were not confined to the eastern half of the Roman Empire. In the course of the fourth century, the allure of the ascetic ideal was felt in the West. Foundations were made on the Italian peninsula, in Gaul and Spain, and along the northern coast of Africa. Martin of Tours was the father of Gallic monasteries. He, too, had a gifted biographer, Sulpicius Severus, whose *Life of Martin* spread the message of the ascetic ideal in the West alongside Athanasius' *Life of Antony*. The inspiration Augustine gave to his foundation in Hippo has lasted to the present. Down through the centuries, his somber and somewhat pessimistic assessment of human nature has provided an authoritative amplification of the theories of Evagrius.

By the fifth century, the golden age had begun to fade. In the East, many monks had become embroiled in doctrinal controversy. Here and there, pederasty cropped up as a debilitating preoccupation in some monastic establishments. In the West, the foundations of Roman civilization weakened under the onslaught of the barbarian tribes, and the ties between the eastern and western halves of the empire began to break apart. Monasteries in Gaul and other parts of the moribund West became refugee cloisters, where monks gathered the few treasures of civilization they could lay hold of in the wake of barbarian pillage. One of these houses was to become especially instrumental in transmitting the traditions of religious life into the future. This was the monastery of Lérins, inauspiciously founded in 405 by Honoratus on an island near Cannes off the southern coast of Gaul. Many monks of this period took to wandering from town to town, begging for more than they needed and making a nuisance of themselves by their uncouth manners and occasional debaucheries. The ascetic ideal went into decline and began to lose its dominance and attractiveness. Some religious simply abandoned their way of life; and many persons wondered if religious life would die out along with the empire, which was in its death throes. However, as dusk settled on the ruins of imperial Rome, the stage was already being set for the rise of feudal Europe and the next age of the evolution of religious life. Out beyond the frontiers of the crumbling empire Celtic monasticism was quietly taking root in far-off Ireland, unnoticed by the bewildered leaders back in the besieged centers of Christianity and the civilized world. The earliest important figure among these first Irish religious was Brigit, the foundress of a monastery at Kildare.

TABLE 1.1: Age of the Desert (200-500)

Dominant Image of Religious Life: The ideal of religious life is the holy ascetic, who seeks the perfection of Christ as a solitary or in community with a group of monks. Disciples withdraw into the "desert" and place themselves under the care of a master ascetic, who teaches them the ways of perfection. They live nearby as hermits or gather in cenobia or monasteries under the leadership of the master. The monk prays, mortifies himself, does battle with the devil for the sake of the Church, and spends his life seeking union with Christ.

Table 1.1—Continued

Second and Third Centuries

100	20,000 Christians in the world	Consecrated virgins and widows
249	Persecution of Decius	live a form of religious life within
251	Antony born	the Christian communities of the
271	Antony withdraws into the desert	early Church during the
292	Pachomius born	persecutions.

Fourth Century

313	Edict of Milan	Hermits and cenobites flourish in
325	Pachomius founds cenobium	the Egyptian desert. Various
356	Antony dies	forms of solitary and community
357	Athanasius writes *Life of Antony*	religious life spread around
360	Basil founds monastery in Cappadocia	eastern rim of the Mediterranean (Palestine, Syria, Cappadocia).
363	Martin founds monastery in Gaul	First monasteries are founded in
376	Melania founds monastery on the Mount of Olives	the West.
389	Simon the Stylite born	
393	Augustine founds monastic group in Hippo	
399	Cassian, disciple of Evagrius, migrates from Egypt to West	

Fifth Century

405	Honoratus founds monastery of Lérins	Religious life continues to expand in the East. While the
410	Alaric sacks Rome	western half of the Roman
415	Cassian founds monastery in Marseilles	Empire crumbles, monastic movement spreads throughout
450	Celtic monasticism takes root in Ireland	the West (Gaul, Spain, Britain, Ireland, etc.).
455	Vandals sack Rome	
459	Simon the Stylite dies	
476	End of the western Roman Empire	
480	Brigit founds double monastery at Kildare	

First Turning Point: *Spread of Benedict's Rule*

The Age of the Desert witnessed the stages of a major era in the history of religious life suggested earlier in this chapter. There was a phase of initial emergence and flourishing growth, which was dominated by a forceful image of what it meant to be a religious; and this image made eminent sense to the Church of that time. This successful phase was followed by a time of turmoil and decline. Finally, a time of change-over ensued as religious life passed through the first major turning point in its history. During the course of this first great age of religious life, its basic patterns emerged clearly. Most of these patterns have remained normative to this day, even though the external shape of religious life has changed drastically. Like the ages that followed it, the Age of the Desert has made a permanent contribution to the heritage that today's religious receive from the past. The stories of Antony, Basil, Pachomius, Melania, Martin, Brigit, and all the other heroic figures of the Age of the Desert are the stories of the first persons to walk down a path that is still followed today.

The Age of Monasticism (500-1200)

The symbolic start of the Age of Monasticism, the next great era in the history of religious life, can be pinpointed with Benedict's founding of Monte Cassino in 529. This monastery, the first to live under the celebrated *Rule* which was to become so important in future centuries, was quite modest in its beginnings. Benedict was not trying to lay the legislative groundwork for the next fifteen centuries or more of religious life. In fact, at the very time that Benedict was guiding the first fledgling Cassinese community through its founding phase, the most important activity in the monastic world was going on in Ireland. Celtic monasticism had landed there some seventy-five years earlier, and was embarking on a period of vigorous growth which stretched across the whole of the sixth century. During that century the Irish Church was gradually transformed from a diocesan and bishop-centered organization to one ruled by the abbots of the network of monasteries which extended across Ireland and had begun, by the end of the century, to reach across the seas. The growth continued through the seventh century and achieved its high level during the eighth, the golden age of the Irish monastic Church. Because of this unique blend of the monastic way of life with the rest of the Irish Church, the leading edge of all of Church history coincides with the history of religious life for the first three centuries of the Age of Monasticism. While the rest of Europe passed through the Dark Ages, the Irish monastic Church attained a high Latin culture of religious and intellectual preeminence, which was the main carrier of the values of Christianity and civilization from the final days of the Roman Empire to the founding centuries of Christendom in the early Middle Ages. This cultural transmission must be viewed as the outstanding accomplishment of Irish religious life.

A special feature of Celtic monasticism was its extremely severe and austere asceticism, which emphasized physical penances. The sturdy Irish monks took this rigor in stride and set their sights on an apostolic ideal which was to become their hallmark. This was the special calling to go into lifetime exile for the sake of the gospels by journeying as missionaries to faraway lands. A good understanding of this ideal is to be had from the exploits of Columban, that most fascinating example of a missionary monk. In his lifetime he was the most brilliant and learned man in all of Europe. It may even be true that Columban is the most influential Irishman who ever lived. He brought Irish culture to the very heartland of Europe and the Christian world, and blazed a trail that would be followed for the next two hundred years by Irish and Anglo-Saxon monks who eventually reached every important center of Christianity.

Columban began his religious life under the direction of a monk of Clonard. While still young, he became convinced that he should become a missionary monk, so he lived for a short time at the monastery of Bangor. From here he journeyed with a party of twelve assistant monks across Britain to what is now northwestern France. There he founded Luxeuil and two other monasteries, whose monks ministered to the people in the Irish fashion and performed some of the functions of the secular clergy. At the same time Columban began a career as teacher and scholar and did not hesitate to denounce improprieties such as the harem kept by the grandson of Queen Brunhilde, the regent of Burgundy. It was not long before Columban got involved in bitter controversies with the local bishops and the queen, who eventually became so angry with him that she exiled him. At first Columban planned to return to Ireland. However, the ship which was to carry him home from the French coast was beaten back by a storm, which Columban took as a sign that he must continue his life as a journeying missionary monk, ever in exile for the sake of the Kingdom. He turned around and went to the Rhineland and Switzerland, where he founded a monastery. After a year he entrusted this house to Gall, one of his faithful followers, and then journeyed south to Bobbio. The monastery which Columban founded there was to become the most important monastery in Italy throughout the eighth and ninth centuries. The spirituality of this monastery maintained a Celtic hue that highlighted a love of nature and wildlife, which may even have influenced young Francis growing up much later in nearby Assisi. From Bobbio, Columban maintained his correspondence with his followers, who by then lived all over Europe. When he died in 615, fifty-three monasteries and convents on the European continent were following his rule, and the reputation of Irish learning was so secure that Irishmen were welcome anywhere in Europe. For the next two centuries Irish learning flowed into Europe and readied Western civilization for the flowering of the High Middle Ages.

When Augustine of Canterbury arrived in Britain at the start of the seventh century, he brought with him a Roman monastic observance, which soon spread across England. By mid-century the wave of Anglo-Saxon monasticism made contact with the Irish Celtic monks, who were moving south from the monastery that Columba founded on the Isle of Iona, off the western coast of Scotland. In Northumbrian monasteries, such as Lindisfarne, the religious vigor and intellectual brilliance of Celtic traditions were fused with the Roman traditions from the south and issued in a style of monastic observance that was a harbinger of the future. Jarrow, another of these Northumbrian monasteries, became at the beginning of the eighth century the home of Venerable Bede, the monk-historian, who would exemplify the monastic ideal for centuries to come. Anglo-Saxon monasticism carried on the missionary traditions of the Irish monks and sent parties to Germany, Scandinavia, Poland, and Bohemia. The most outstanding among these missionaries was Boniface, who planted the Benedictine seed in Germany in 744.

The centuries of Celtic monastic ascendancy were also the centuries of the gradual but steady spread of Benedict's *Rule*. When Benedict composed the *Rule*, it was intended only for the small house of Monte Cassino. He was familiar with the wisdom of the desert and carefully culled from its many traditions those which he thought best suited for a religious life to be led amid the unsettled conditions of the sixth-century Italian countryside. In the process, he produced the germ of a new dominant image of religious life. This image was not only a correction of the abuses which had crept in during the decline of the Age of the Desert; it also, and more importantly, turned out to be a successful adaptation of the ascetic ideal to the feudal society which emerged from the Dark Ages and reached its crest in the early medieval period. Benedict's short and practical *Rule* furnished workable guidelines for all monastic activity and every age and class of monks. It combined an uncompromising spirituality with physical moderation and flexibility. It emphasized the charity and harmony of a simple life in common under the guidance of a wise and holy abbot. Monastic wanderlust was checked by stability. The excellence of the eremitical ideal of the past was acknowledged and duly praised, but it was recommended only for those religious who were advanced in perfection.

At the start of the sixth century, the vision of religious life contained in Benedict's Rule was just one among a great variety of regimes, which varied in austerity, thrust, and rigor of observance. Some leaned toward an ideal of harsh asceticism;

others, toward a communal life blended with a cultivation of study. In this context, Benedict's Rule began its gradual expansion. It was adopted, one monastery at a time, without being imposed by any higher authority. Sometimes newly founded monasteries adopted the Rule, and in other cases it was taken on by established monasteries that desired a change of discipline. As time went on, the myth grew up that all monasteries had in one way or another derived from Monte Cassino. By the time of Charlemagne, almost all monasteries followed Benedict's Rule, and some chroniclers wondered if there had been any monks in Europe prior to Benedict. Charlemagne's son, Louis, sought to regularize and reform monasticism by decreeing that Benedict's Rule be observed by all the monasteries of his realms. Benedict of Aniane was the principal coordinator of this effort, even though it did not achieve lasting success after the Carolingian era had passed its peak. A successful unification of all monasteries did not occur until the great monastery of Cluny began its impressive growth in the tenth century. Through the tenth and eleventh centuries the Cluniac federation grew in size, strength, and influence. Cluniac ideals became the model for Christian spirituality, the Cluniac network was used to bolster papal strength, and the Cluniac system of more than a thousand monasteries prefigured the structures of a religious order of later centuries.

By the end of the eleventh century, the Cluniac network had become vast, wealthy, and, to some, a source of scandal. During this century various attempts were made to restore the primitive fervor of the Benedictine ideal. Chief among these were the Carthusian and Cistercian reforms. The Carthusians, like the Camaldolese and a few other groups of this period, fashioned their reform on a semi-eremitical life style. The Cistercians, on the other hand, sought to divest themselves of the pomp and splendor which they felt had come to encrust the Cluniacs and return to the literal observance of Benedict's Rule down to the last jot and tittle. Despite this intention, they did manage to introduce a series of fortunate innovations into religious life, especially under the forceful leadership of Bernard. Since men's religious life was becoming increasingly clericalized by this period, the Cistercians invented a new category of membership, that of the lay brothers, who devoted their lives to manual labor and did not bother learning to read. Another practical invention was the General Chapter, a further step toward the governing apparatus of the modern religious order. During the twelfth century the Cistercians expanded rapidly. Before long though, they also became successful and rich in land.

As the twelfth century ran its course, various ferments of change were being felt in society, the Church, and the religious life. The first stirrings of urbanization emerged with the growth of medieval towns. Because of the Crusades and the beginnings of world trade, contacts were made with Arab civilization and through it with the classical learning of antiquity. Somehow, the many monasteries which dotted the European countryside and had proved to be so successful in the ways of feudal culture began to appear inadequate in the face of these movements. Once again laxity in religious life was not uncommon. There was also a readiness to engage in petty contention, such as the debate that went on between monks and canons about which of their forms of religious life was a more authentic embodiment of the apostolic ideal. For a long time the monks felt that their celibacy was superior to the lifestyle of the secular clergy who often married. Through the centuries of the early medieval period, the canons, who emerged from the secular clergy, sought to remedy this supposed inferiority by requiring celibacy more and more. In fact, celibacy became mandatory for all the secular clergy in 1139. Furthermore, the canons maintained that the priesthood made them superior to the monks, many of whom were laymen. This contention gradually led to the virtually complete clericalization of the monks and the relegation of male lay religious to a subordinate category in the monasteries. This debate was not fully settled until the following century with the rise of the mendicants, who blended the best features of the lifestyles of both the monks and the canons into their new form of religious life.

TABLE 1.2: Age of Monasticism (500-1200)

Dominant Image of Religious Life: Life in a monastery under the discipline of the holy Rule is the ideal of the religious. The daily round of liturgical prayer, work, and contemplation provides a practical setting to pursue the lofty goals of unceasing praise of God and union with Christ. Within the Church and society, monks and nuns set an example of how deep spirituality can be combined with loving ministry to one's neighbor and dutiful fidelity to the concrete tasks of daily life.

Sixth Century

515 Finnian founds Clonard	Rapid expansion of Celtic monas-
529 Benedict founds Monte Cassino	ticism in Ireland. Various rules
563 Columba founds Iona	observed in monasteries of Gaul
577 Lombards destroy Monte Cassino	and Italy.
591 Columban founds Luxeuil	
'596 Augustine of Canterbury sent to Britain	

Seventh and Eighth Centuries

613 Columban founds Bobbio	Religious life of North Africa
635 Bobbio adopts Benedict's Rule	wiped out by Moslem expansion.
640 Aiden founds Lindisfarne	Missionary journeys of Celtic
642 Arab conquest of Egypt	monks to evangelize Europe and
664 Synod of Whitby fuses Celtic and Anglo-Saxon observance	revive learning in the Church. Golden age of Irish monastic
665 Luxeuil adopts Benedict's Rule	Church. Gradual spread of Bene-
717 Monte Cassino refounded	dict's Rule to more and more
735 Venerable Bede dies at Jarrow	European monasteries and
744 Boniface founds Fulda	convents.
755 Chrodegang writes rule for canons	

Ninth Century

816 *Regula Canonicorum* of Aix-la-Chapelle	Observance of canons regular is made uniform by spread of the
817 Louis of France decrees that Benedict's Rule be observed throughout Carolingian realms; Benedict of Aniane coordinates this policy	*Regula* of Aix. Consolidation of Benedict's Rule; virtually all of religious life becomes "Benedictine."

Table 1.2—Continued

Tenth and Eleventh Centuries

910 Cluniac reform	Various reforms breathe new life
1015 Camaldolese reform	into Benedict's ideal and intro-
1084 Carthusian reform	duce organizational variations.
1098 Cistercian reform	

Twelfth Century

1111 Bernard joins the Cistercians	Canons regular unite into orders,
1119 Templars founded	which are a variation of the
1120 Premonstratensians founded	monastic networks of Cluny and
1135 Gilbertines founded	Cîteaux. Military orders attempt
1190 Teutonic Knights founded	a new form of religious life which
	is temporarily successful.

Second Turning Point: *Rise of the Mendicants*

Another sign that the religious life of the twelfth century was groping to find new directions is evident in the experiments that were made to combine the life of the monk with that of the soldier in the military orders. These ventures, which grew in part out of the medieval zeal for crusading, had a short-lived success. The Templars are a good example of the phenomenon. They were founded to protect the holy places that had been wrested from Arab control by Crusade victory, and to keep these places safe for European pilgrims. At the start the Templars accomplished their task well. They established a system of outposts which watched over the principal pilgrimage routes and served as guides for the pilgrims. They set up houses in the principal cities of Europe, where they helped to organize pilgrimages and send them on their way to the Holy Land. The Templars even devised an ingenious method to protect the pilgrims' money from theft.

Pilgrims could deposit the money at a Templar house in some European city such as London or Paris, where they were issued certificates of deposit. Upon their arrival in Jerusalem, they redeemed the certificates for the deposited amount minus a slight interest charge for the service, which was kept by the Templars. In this manner the Templars hit on a technique of funds transfer which foreshadowed modern banking. It was not long before merchants, who plied the new trade routes to the East, were availing themselves of the Templars' service alongside the holy pilgrims. Soon the service charges which the Templars kept began to accumulate, and as the thirteenth century wore on the order became one of the richest institutions of medieval Europe. This wealth lead to a laxity amongst the brothers, many of whom had lost sight of their founding purpose. No doubt this wealth was one of the causes which brought about the suppression of the Templars by Rome right after the end of the thirteenth century.

In the seven centuries of the Age of Monasticism, it is once again possible to discern in broad outline the typical features of a major era in the history of religious life. The entire age was dominated by an image of the monk or nun spending a lifetime in a monastery or abbey under the observance of a holy rule. During the sixth and seventh centuries, European convents and monasteries observed a variety of such rules, the most important of which were the various versions of Celtic discipline. At the same time, Benedict's more temperate approach began its gradual expansion, took the lead in the eighth century, and emerged as the dominant pattern from the ninth to the twelfth centuries. During these last four centuries of the Age of Monasticism, reform of religious life always involved some sort of return to Benedict's Rule. In fact, to this day religious life in the Western Church looks to Benedict as its patriarch and one of its wisest teachers. Finally, in the last century of the Age of Monasticism, it became clear that some sort of change-over was beginning, as religious life sought to adapt to new conditions in the Church and society.

The Age of the Mendicant Orders (1200-1500)

When Francis and Dominic launched their communities in the early thirteenth century, they ushered in the next major era in the history of religious life, the Age of the Mendicant Orders. The mendicant ideal pulled together some of the variations that had cropped up in the previous century and fused them with the central objectives of religious life. Begging for alms was the linchpin which creatively and successfully held together all these diverse features. By divesting themselves of landed wealth, the mendicants provided the Church with a fresh example of what it could mean to be evangelically poor. This example contrasted vividly with the communal landed wealth of the established monastic orders and with the newer monetary wealth of the Templars. Religious life had always espoused the individual renunciation of personal ownership; in this regard, the mendicants were quite traditional. But over the centuries communal ownership by monastic orders had periodically accumulated to the point of obscuring the witness of gospel poverty. For almost the whole of the thirteenth century, the mendicants were able to maintain their communal wealth at such a low level that they succeeded in adding an extra meaning to religious poverty, which still inspires all religious down to the present day. Furthermore, without being tied down to monasteries, which by this time had become vast feudal estates, the mendicants could intentionally embrace the apostolic mobility which was truly needed in the Church, but which was then considered incompatible with the ideal of monastic stability. This sort of mobility had been achieved as an exception by leading individuals such as Bernard, or as a side effect of the objectives of the orders of canons or the military orders. The mendicants, however, deliberately renounced communal wealth to attain this sort of mobility. This mobility, which resulted from begging alms, also suited the mendicants well for serving the new needs of medieval society and Church. They could set up priories in the new

TABLE 1.3: Age of the Mendicant Orders (1200-1500)

Dominant Image of Religious Life: The simple friar who begs for his keep and follows in the footsteps of the Lord is the idea of religious life and medieval Christendom. He prays as he goes, steeping himself in the love of Christ. Unencumbered by landed wealth, the mendicants are free to travel on foot to any place they are needed by the Church and to provide it with a credible example of the gospel injunction to give away everything to the poor. They hold themselves ready to preach, cultivate learning, serve the poor, and minister to the needs of society in the name of the Church.

Thirteenth Century

1207	Dominicans founded	Rapid expansion of mendicant
1209	Carmelites founded	orders. Friaries and priories
1211	Franciscans founded	spring up in medieval towns
1216	Beguines begin	across Europe. Mendicants teach,
1221	5,000 Franciscans attend chapter of Mats	especially in the new universities, and preach, especially against
1243	Augustinians founded	heresy. Monastic orders imitate
1256	13,000 Dominicans in world	some activities of the mendicants.
1298	Boniface VIII imposes cloister on all women religious	

Fourteenth Century

1312	Templars suppressed by Rome	Stabilization and slow decline of
1325	75,000 men in mendicant orders	mendicant orders. Flagrant
1344	Brigittines founded	abuses and laxity are prevalent
1349	Black Death	in religious life during the last
1365	Alexian Brothers founded	half of the century
1400	47,000 men in mendicant orders	

Fifteenth Century

1415	Hus burned at the stake	Various reforms restore the
1435	Minims founded	mendicant ideal and produce a
1450	Gutenberg	gradual increase in membership.
1492	Columbus	First stirrings of the
1500	90,000 men in mendicant orders	Renaissance introduce an uneasiness into the Church and religious life.

Third Turning Point: *The Counter-Reformation*

medieval towns that were fast turning into centers of medieval culture and life. The mendicants thus positioned themselves to help the Church in a new and effective way to do its teaching and preaching mission. During the previous centuries this teaching and preaching mission had been considered the job and responsibility of the secular clergy and more recently the canons regular, who were seen as semireligious. Now the mendicants, who were striving to be religious in the full sense, were also able to participate in the central functions of the Church's hierarchical mission.

This constellation of factors accounts in part for the mendicants' rapid expansion and success, which has to be judged spectacular by almost any standards. The Dominicans, for example, grew to a membership of thirteen thousand in just forty years. The Franciscans grew even more rapidly. While it is true, of course, that the vast majority of religious in the thirteenth century still belonged to the monastic orders, none of the old orders experienced such spectacular rates of growth. As mendicant priories, friaries, and convents sprang up across Europe, they met with an initial hostility from those who could not fathom how this new lifestyle could be an authentic form of religious life. Another source of hostility was the mendicants' external resemblance to fanatical and heretical sects of the time, such as the Waldensians, the Humiliati, and the Cathars. This confusion was no doubt eventually overcome by the strong sense of loyalty to the hierarchy and adherence to its orthodox teachings which both Dominic and Francis instilled in their sons and daughters. Gradually, the new image of religious life became acceptable, and proved to be a much better adaptation of religious life to the needs of the emerging urban society than was possible from monasteries in their isolated rural settings. During the course of the thirteenth century, even the monastic orders established *studia* close to the new universities where the mendicants were flourishing. As Christendom reached its zenith, the image of a new kind of religious life unencumbered by landed wealth played a key role in the

Church's spirituality, the cultivation of the intellectual life of the Church and society, and in the preaching of the gospel for the Church.

After a rapid flowering, the mendicant orders were affected by the same changes that spread across the Church and European society in the fourteenth and fifteenth centuries. The fourteenth century is perhaps the period of the most flagrant laxity in the entire history of religious life. The mendicants, who had been founded in reaction to the decadence of monastic wealth, succumbed with even greater flair to the same evil. In a legalistic manner, for example, mendicant friars took note that their rule forbade serving meat in the refectories of their houses. So they made arrangements to have their cells expanded into small apartments, where meat could be served. When priories were established, provision was made for this kind of expansion of each cell. Rear entrances were built into each apartment to allow cooks to enter and prepare meals for the friars, since the rule did not allow laymen to pass through the front entrances and into the cloister. It was also in this era that the *peculium* became popular in religious life. This was an annual allowance of money which religious with solemn vows could spend without giving an account of it each time. Arrangements could be made to increase the size of this allotment, in some cases, for the religious who came from a noble or otherwise wealthy family. Members of monastic orders, who were imitating the mendicants in so many other ways, also adopted this custom. These extra funds were used at times for all manner of extravagance and diversion. Monks and friars arranged to have special habits sewn for themselves, which were lined with silk and sported extra cuffs, pleats, and buttons. Seamstresses were engaged to sew these habits; they could use the rear entrances to the cells of the religious to come to do the sewing, and often they were asked to linger for amorous interludes. Women's religious life at this time came up with its own special forms of laxity. One abuse which was especially common was lap dogs. Women used their funds to vie with each other in making elaborately embroidered and bejeweled cushions with long silk ribbons. On these cushions they placed their pet dogs, which they held in their laps while they recited the psalms in choir.

These internal laxities were only one source of difficulty for religious life in the late Middle Ages. Halfway through the fourteenth century, religious life was dealt a very severe blow by the Black Death. Large numbers of religious died. Those who did die were in many cases the more pious and devout religious, because it was these very religious who went into the towns to care for the general population afflicted by the disease. As a result, the religious who survived the plague included a disproportionate number of less generous individuals.

While these external and internal disorganizing forces acted directly on religious life, the pressure of larger social change began to mount throughout Europe. As the Renaissance brought a new humanism and the secularization of European society, and various other movements hinted at the coming breakup of Christendom, a malaise was clearly descending upon the Church and religious life. The overall impression which religious gave on the eve of the Reformation was, to say the least, uninspiring. Once again it seemed that the time was ripe for a new regeneration and revitalization of religious life.

The Age of the Apostolic Orders (1500-1800)

The next major era in the history of religious life, the Age of the Apostolic Orders, was heralded by two new foundations in the first half of the sixteenth century: the Ursulines and the Jesuits. To better understand the new direction these foundations were taking, it is necessary to recall the far-ranging changes that were transforming all of European society. The medieval world was gone. The new humanism ushered in with the Renaissance during the previous century laid the groundwork for the rational bent of the modern era dawning upon Europe. On all sides new possibilities were seen for humankind. The New World had just been discovered. Printing was making widespread learning a true possibility. The optimism for human potential stood in stark contrast to a generally low opinion of the decadent condition of the Church. Religious life did not escape this disrespect, since the modest reform efforts of the fifteenth century did not change the impression of laxity religious life had made in the late Middle Ages. Religious life was in a precarious position, as was the Church as a whole. It was in this situation that Luther precipitated the Protestant revolt, which had as one of its first effects the virtual elimination of religious life throughout the countries of Europe that became Protestant.

Considering the cases of the Jesuits and Ursulines in turn will shed light on the new directions taken by religious in response to these large-scale changes in society and the Church. From the very start, the Jesuits claimed as theirs the ideal of excellence for the sake of the Lord God: excellence in sanctity and holiness, excellence in the intellectual life, excellence in apostolic zeal, whether it concerned extirpating the heresies of Protestantism to regain the wayward flock, or carrying the message of faith on missionary journeys to the very antipodes. With just a year of training at the hands of Ignatius, Francis Xavier was ready to set out for the mission of the Far East, where he spent the rest of his life. The intense personal formation of the Jesuits in disciplined pursuit of holiness allowed these new militant servants of the Pope to do without the safeguards of regular monastic observance, such as daily singing of the communal office in choir. Instead they immersed themselves in the exercise of individual meditation, the new format of prayer that reflected the new philosophical bent of the emerging modern era. In contrast to the medieval presupposition that the whole is a mysterious unity of parts and yet somehow more than any one of its parts or the conjunction of all its parts, the pioneers of the modern era dedicated themselves to see how far they could go with the proposition that the whole is just the sum of its separate parts, each of which is simple and available for rational examination. The new prayer style of meditation was an uninterrupted parcel of time given over to mental prayer and separate from the other activities of the religious; the apostolate in turn was also considered to be separate, as were other components of this new religious lifestyle. Taken together, these individual components equipped the new religious for renewing the Church in response to the challenge of the Reformation, shoring up the Church's political power in Catholic Europe, preaching the gospel in foreign missions to the newly discovered lands, and coming to grips with the secularizing trends of the scientific revolution, modern philosophy, and the rise of nationalism in Europe. Jesuits, for example, could be found blazing trails and setting precedents for the missionary conquests of the Church, negotiating on the Church's behalf at the royal courts of almost all of Europe's Catholic kingdoms, learning the new physics in the laboratories of the new scientists, and teaching the youthful Descartes at their school in La Flèche.

Among the women religious, the Ursulines also exemplified clearly the new thrust of religious life. Angela Merici centered her new foundation on apostolic service. Once again, personal holiness is seen as the only dependable agency of reform; the same push for excellence is not there, but there is still emphasis on individual holiness. The primitive Ursulines were so different from the cloistered nuns of their time that they bear a close resemblance to what is today called a secular institute. Initially, they lived in their homes and formed a loose-knit company of virgins devoted to assisting the poor and caring for the infirm in the style of their foundress. Their reputation for truly holy and exemplary service spread rapidly. Shortly after Angela's death, the Ursulines came under the systematizing influence of Charles Borromeo, who was zealous to enforce the Tridentine structures of reform. He was one among many ecclesiastics who took note of the fact that the newly founded Ursulines aspired to a form of life that was religious and yet did not live in cloister, in violation of the new decrees of the Council of Trent which imposed cloister on all nuns and punished violations of this cloister with excommunication. Pius V had just promulgated a decree which restated and reemphasized the necessity of cloister for all nuns. While it is true that Charles Borromeo never forced the Ursulines to retire behind cloister walls, he did encourage them to live in community rather than separately with their families. By the time the Ursulines expanded to France in the seventeenth century, pressure to attain the status of true nuns with solemn vows was so intense that arrangements were made to obtain papal approval for having the new foundation of Paris Ursulines take vows and become cloistered nuns. To accomplish this change some of the apostolic flexibility of the original foundation was curtailed.

Even though the new image of religious life succeeded in freeing the religious for apostolic mobility and carried on the apostolic direction which the mendicants had already begun in the Middle Ages, the churchmen of the sixteenth century still could not conceive of a true religious life for women that was not cloistered. However, the impulse toward the apostolate was so strong that in the course of the seventeenth and eighteenth centuries more and more women found ways of doing the apostolate without being confined to the cloister. At the start of the seventeenth century, Francis de Sales had tried to obtain this option for the Order of Visitation nuns he was founding. But even this prestigious prelate could not overcome the insistence of his metropolitan that the Visitation nuns be cloistered. Perhaps it was the contact of Vincent de Paul with Jane Frances de Chantal, after the death of Francis, that led Vincent to try a different approach with his Daughters of Charity. He insisted with them that they were not religious and that they should never strive to be such, for then they would have to become cloistered and cease their apostolic activity, and this would mean they would cease being true Daughters of Charity. The St. Joseph Sisters, who were destined to become one of the largest congregations of women in the Church after the French Revolution, were founded at the midpoint of the sixteenth century. They succeeded in being apostolic and evading the cloister. Perhaps this was due simply to the fact that their small size (at most one hundred or so sisters prior to the Revolution) made them inconspicuous enough to avoid the pressures to become cloistered.

Another characteristic of the Age of the Apostolic Orders, which has had lasting effects on religious life to this day, is the fact that France at that time reached the zenith of its cultural leadership in Europe. The thrust toward the apostolate for women centered in France. As France replaced Spain as Europe's major Catholic political power, so leadership in setting the style of missionary work was taken over by the French. French Jesuits and French Ursulines set the pace of missionary work in the New World in the seventeenth century, eclipsing the Spaniards. The great masters of the French School of spirituality devised an approach to the spiritual life which was passed on almost unchanged to the next age in the history of religious life. This spirituality emphasized values of the Christian tradition passed over since medieval times and joined them to a mistrust of human nature which took exception to the humanist optimism of the period. This mistrust took an even more dour form among the Jansenists, another French contribution that exerted an influence well into the nineteenth and twentieth centuries, long after their formal condemnation by the Church. Finally, it should be pointed out that France was a center of the Enlightenment in the final years of the Age of the Apostolic Orders. This rationalist movement challenged the very existence and basis of the Church, and of religious life as well.

During the eighteenth century, a slow decline began in religious life. Large but nearly empty religious houses could be found almost everywhere in Europe. The Enlightenment undermined the rationale for religious life, and many liberated religious seemed to agree with this new thinking as they attended meetings of anticlericalists at Freemason lodges or discussions with Enlightenment savants in the salons of Paris. The Bourbon kings succeeded in persuading Rome to suppress the Jesuits in 1773. On the eve of the French Revolution, worldwide membership in all the men's religious orders stood at approximately 300,000; by the time the Revolution and the secularizations which followed had run their course in France and the rest of Europe, fewer than 70,000 remained. Many orders passed out of existence—some were suppressed by the state, while others simply closed down after the majority of their members had departed. The few scattered religious who remained were old and shell-shocked. Some prophets of doom predicted the demise of religious life as a whole. In fact, the way had been cleared for a revival and recovery of religious life.

TABLE 1.4: Age of the Apostolic Orders (1500-1800)

Dominant Image of Religious Life: Men and women religious are to form an elite corps of devoted servants ready to aid the Church in its new apostolic needs, especially the formidable renewal tasks of the Counter-Reformation. A high level of personal holiness enables these religious to face the risks of these new undertakings without the protection of all the monastic observances.

Sixteenth Century

1517	Luther sparks the Reformation	Religious life virtually wiped out in Protestant Europe. Founding and spread of a new style of religious life in the format of orders dedicated to the active apostolate, with no enclosure in the case of women. These groups work at providing services of charity and instruction, shoring up the Church's political power in Catholic Europe, and spreading the gospel in the foreign missions.
1535	Ursulines founded	
1539	Gilbertines suppressed by Henry VIII	
1540	Jesuits founded	
1541	Francis Xavier sails for the Far East	
1545	Trent starts	
1561	Teutonic Knights disband	
1562	Discalced Carmelite reform	
1563	Trent imposes cloister on all nuns under pain of excommunication	

Table 1.4—Continued

Seventeenth Century

1610	Visitation Nuns founded
1625	Vincentians founded
1633	Daughters of Charity founded
1650	St. Joseph Sisters founded
1662	Rancé launches Trappist reform
1663	Paris Foreign Mission Society founded
1681	Christian Brothers founded
1700	213,000 men in mendicant orders

Flowering of Baroque spirituality, especially in French School. Adaptation for the sake of the apostolate spawns new variations: societies of priests and clerical congregations for men; more or less successful attempts to evade cloister for women. Bulk of men religious still belong to mendicant orders.

Eighteenth Century

1720	Passionists founded
1735	Redemptorists founded
1770	300,000 men in religious life in world
1773	Jesuits suppressed by Rome
1789	French Revolution starts

A few new congregations are founded but religious life as a whole seems to be in slow decline due to mentality of the Enlightenment, inroads of Jansenism, enervation of comfort and wealth. Weakened religious life is delivered the *coup de grâce* by the French Revolution, which sets off a wave of political suppression and defection in France and across the rest of Catholic Europe.

Fourth Turning Point: *French Revolution*

The Age of the Teaching Congregations (1800-Present)

The revival of religious life which occurred in the next period, the Age of the Teaching Congregations, set off in a new direction. About six hundred new communities were founded in the nineteenth century. For the most part, these groups were dedicated to the ideal of building institutions and having their members selflessly apply themselves to attaining the professional standards required for excellence in those institutions. This kind of dedication called for great emphasis on the virtues of humility and simplicity, which became the hallmark virtues for religious in the new congregations. The pursuit of holiness came to be seen as a humble and simple dedication to a community's institutions, so that those institutions could become acceptable by secular standards and at the same time be apostolic tools suited to the new needs of the Church. The most widespread instance of this strategy was the enlistment of religious communities in the movement of educating the masses. For the first time in European history, the idea of educating everyone had the possibility of being realized. The new congregations joined in this movement in hopes of planting the seeds of a robust faith in the souls of the children they taught—by the thousands. Zeal for the education of children combined with the refurbished spirituality of the seventeenth century to form the motivational underpinning of the new-style religious. Their activities spilled over into other apostolic works such as hospitals, but teaching was the paradigm. Even the few pre-Revolution orders which were managing a slow recovery took on many of the trappings of the typical nineteenth-century teaching congregation. For the first time in the history of religious life, recruitment of adult vocations was almost completely displaced by candidates just emerging from childhood.

The reasons religious life took this new turn have to do with the fact that the Church became aware that it could really get in contact with masses of people and show them Christianity precisely by using the institutions emerging at this time. The institution became a means of Christianizing. The impact of this vision can be clarified by contrasting it with the role assigned to schools by Jesuits two hundred years earlier. In the seventeenth century Jesuits opened, developed, and perfected a type of secondary school primarily designed to teach sons of noblemen. This kind of school was a means of getting in touch with influential people. The Jesuits of that period subscribed to the proposition that the Church and the world could be affected by influencing influential people. This seventeenth-century Jesuit education aimed at the elite: the education of the nineteenth-century teaching congregations aimed at the masses. Both kinds of education strove to complement the Church's ordinary ministry. Religious still saw themselves as bishops' specialized auxiliaries working at the tasks that the secular clergy could not handle in its ordinary parish ministry. The difference in the nineteenth century lay in the large role played by women and the value ascribed to humble and devoted service by individuals willingly and generously submerging themselves to the ends of apostolic institutions.

Through the end of the nineteenth century and on into the twentieth, the religious who gave themselves to the demanding work of schools and hospitals edified the Church and produced a brand of holiness appropriate for a Catholicism which sought to bolster a papacy denuded of worldly power and to care for the huddled masses of the industrialized world that needed re-Christianization. By the middle of the present century, the vast network of Catholic institutions staffed by increasingly professional religious spanned the developed countries and reached out to the missionary lands. The system worked well and had been fine-tuned for maximum effect.

This well-working system pulled together in a remarkably satisfying way various trends and potentialities of the Church of the Counter-Reformation which had not had a chance to develop before the French Revolution or which had been violently disrupted by the Revolution and its aftershocks. To begin with, the feudal structures within which religious life had been embedded since the dawn of Europe were finally discarded as an unneeded carapace. Instead of each monastery, convent, friary, priory, or other religious establishment being a benefice to which a guaranteed fixed annual income was attached, it now turned out to be the case that religious communities were cut loose and had to find a new practical means of support. The governments of the nineteenth century, Catholic or otherwise, avoided state support of religious orders in every way they could because of the success of those ideas of the Age of Reason which dictated that the only legitimate role of religious was secular service to society. In nineteenth-century France, for example, an association committed to grade-school teaching could be subsidized as such. If, however, that same association were also a religious congregation, it was entitled to no state support on that account. As a religious congregation it had no legal status in the country. Even though this course of events was resisted by the conservative churchmen of the day, who were trying unsuccessfully to reestablish the Church in the pattern of pre-Revolutionary times, the course of events had a momentum that was too strong to resist. The pattern turned out to be a blessing in disguise, since it meant that the apostolic method which Vincent de Paul and John Baptist de la Salle had experimented with on a limited scale in the seventeenth century was now adopted across the board. Just as the spirituality of the masters of the French School flowered two hundred years later within the nascent teaching congregations of the nineteenth century, so the apostolic technique of reaching masses of the poor through an institutionalized approach to the works of mercy turned into the near-universal method of the nineteenth century. This turn of events had the unexpected benefit of providing a fresh inspiration for the Church in the example of religious "poorly" serving the poor. Prior to the French Revolution the well-endowed and well-financed religious orders had an appearance of such lax indulgence that it was doubted whether religious orders would ever again inspire the faithful by the example of living in poverty. After the Revolution, religious orders had no choice. The means of security in the past had been taken away, never to be returned, and the demands of day-to-day living forced a poor lifestyle on the new congregations.

About the time of the Second Vatican Council, membership in religious communities had reached the highest point in the history of the Church, surpassing even the maximums

---

TABLE 1.5: Age of the Teaching Congregations (1800-Present)

Dominant Image of Religious Life: Religious dedicate their lives to the salvation of their own souls and the salvation of others. The style of life of religious men and women blends an intense pursuit of personal holiness with a highly active apostolic service. Identity with the person of Christ unites this twofold objective into a single purpose.

Nineteenth Century

1814	French Restoration; Jesuits restored by Rome	Revival of religious life after widespread state suppressions. Numerous foundations of congregations dedicated to a return to authentic religious life blended with service, principally in schools. Old orders, such as Jesuits and Dominicans, rejuvenated in the format of the teaching congregations. Church gradually centralizes around the papacy and isolates itself from secular trends of the modern world.
1825	Fewer than 70,000 men in religious life in world	
1831	Mercy Sisters founded	
1850	83,000 men in religious life in world	
1859	Salesians founded	
1870	Papal infallibility declared	

Twentieth Century

1901	*Normae* recognized noncloistered women as true religious	Expansion and solidification. In the sixties, crises set in from within religious life due to loss of identity and inroads of secularizing process. Numerous defections and decreasing numbers of new members.
1962	Vatican II: 173,351 women and 33,309 men in religious life in U.S.	
1966	181,411 women and 35,029 men in religious life in U.S.	
1977	130,804 women and 30,960 men in religious life in U.S.	

Fifth Turning Point: (?)

---

that had been achieved before the French Revolution. In the last decade this trend reversed for the first time in a century and a half. Large numbers of religious withdrew from the life and recruitment figures plummeted. Some ascribe this crisis to a loss of identity and an internal weakening of religious life by the absorption of secular values and patterns. It seems that another turning point in the long history of religious life has begun. Major shifts seem to be moving society and culture, and the Church itself is negotiating a new course on which it was set by the changes inaugurated at Vatican II.

Some Limitations and Generalizations

Limitations

Before proceeding, some concluding and cautionary remarks must be made. The rapid overview of the history of religious life given in this chapter should not be taken as anything more than a demonstration of how the evolution of religious life can be interpreted so as to fit the model of the five main eras that are being postulated in the proposed historical model. The account is far too compressed and oversimplified to provide an adequate and properly nuanced telling of the story of religious life. For example, little attention was given to the canons regular, who constituted a significant portion of men religious from the Middle Ages to the French Revolution. There was no discussion of the medieval military orders nor of Orthodox monasticism. A still more gaping lacuna is the sketchy analysis of the way women's religious life differed from or followed the same pattern as that of the men. It may be that the sources used in this study were not sensitive to the distinctive role women actually played in the evolution of religious life. On the other hand, it may be that up to the present time the trends of women's religious life have been parallel to those in the men's orders.

Generalizations

The model presented in the previous section suggests some generalized conclusions. These conclusions can be helpful in exploring the present crisis of religious life.

The historical evidence suggests that there have been significant shifts in the dominant image of religious life across the centuries. These shifts seem to occur when there are major societal changes astir and when the Church too is undergoing major changes. The first transition happened as the Roman Empire fell in the West and feudal Europe was beginning; at the same time the rift between western and eastern Christianity was starting. The second transition occurred as feudal Europe was giving way to medieval urbanization and as the Church was gathering all of Europe into the unity of Christendom. The third transition took place at the start of the modern period of Western civilization as the Church underwent the shock of the Reformation. The fourth transition resulted from a direct attack of society on the Church as a whole and on religious life in particular. Admittedly each of these changes in the culture and the Church differed from one another in many respects. However, the pattern seems clear enough to permit one to ask whether perhaps another shift in the dominant image of religious life would happen if major changes in society and the Church should come to pass.

Although religious communities have been founded in almost every century of Christian history, it seems that each major shift in the dominant image of religious life is heralded by some significantly new foundations which embody a new image in an especially striking way. This could be said of the earliest Benedictine monasteries for the first transition, of the Franciscans and Dominicans for the second transition, of the Jesuits and Ursulines for the third transition, and of the plethora of nineteenth-century foundations for the fourth transition. It also seems to be the case that many communities go out of existence at each transition. Those that survive either continue in a diminished form or somehow blend the new dominant image with the charism of their own foundation to get another lease on life. The mendicant orders, for example, grew numerically stronger during the Age of Apostolic Orders as they adapted their own special gifts to the new style of religious life. The culture of the High Middle Ages was rapidly and irretrievably passing away, but the mendicants adapted and flourished. One might ask, then, if the Church would witness the death of many religious communities and the foundation of new and different ones if a shift in the dominant image of religious life were to occur. A premise for this book is the plausibility of maintaining that another major transition has in fact begun in the history of religious life. Should this hypothesis be true, it would be appropriate to pose questions about how religious life is dying and how a recovery and revitalization might happen.

Another observation that suggests itself from this brief survey concerns the continuity that underlies the shifts of the dominant image of religious life. As the image evolves it continues to hold up the compelling idea of a radical following of the conditions set forth by Christ for an evangelical discipleship embedded in a life of prayer and deep faith. While the contemporary religious would probably not feel called to take on the externals of the life of the ascetics of the Age of the Desert, he or she will surely understand and be drawn to the stark beauty of the life of radical discipleship that moved Antony to withdraw into the desert. Similar remarks could probably be made about the ultimate aims of the first Franciscans and the first rugged band of Jesuits. Through all the twists and turns in the makeup and style of religious life, there is a deep core of seeking union with Christ in a special and total way that endures century after century. A great deal of historical precedent would have to be explained away by anyone who would wish to maintain that religious life is about to disappear as a separate and distinguishable way of life in the Church. The historical pattern seems to be one of repeated recovery. The present moment is indeed a time of trouble for religious communities, but religious life as a whole will doubtlessly survive.

Where Does Religious Life Stand Today?

In the previous sections of this chapter, the history of the religious-life movement in the Church was examined to determine the major factors within culture, the Church, and religious life itself that significantly influence the evolution of this movement. Generalizations from the proposed historical model indicate that major turning points are likely to occur in religious life when both the Church and secular culture are in the midst of major changes and when religious life itself is disoriented by upheaval. As was mentioned in the introduction, a central conjecture being proposed in this book is that religious life is undergoing a pervasive transition that will last for the next twenty to twenty-five years and which will significantly change the life and service of religious communities before it has run its full course. The plausibility of this conjecture rests in part on the definite possibility that the necessary changes in the religious life, the Church, and in society and culture are at hand today.

Crisis in the Church and Religious Life

The Catholic Church in America has been profoundly influenced by contemporary change. For at least fifteen years the Church has been experiencing a transition of its life. The Second Vatican Council (1962-64) was a result of the early stages of this transition and a triggering event for its later stages. The Church began to open itself to a world which was undergoing a dramatic secularization. This opening up, or *aggiornamento*, had significant impact on all dimensions of Church life. Parish life and parochial education are no longer the only shapers of the values and beliefs of American Catholics. The once-clear norms and social roles within the Church no longer seem to serve their original purpose. For example, the Vatican's official position on birth control is considered unacceptable to an increasingly large number of Catholics.

Difficulties are arising in the functioning of such Church structures as the priesthood and the traditional role of the laity and of such Church institutions as parishes, schools, and hospitals. Their once-unquestioned role within the Church no longer seems to satisfy the needs of an increasingly large number of church members.

This crisis and transition within the Church has had a dramatic effect on religious communities of women and men.

Religious communities have begun to experience all of the signs of entering into the breakdown and disintegration period described earlier in this chapter. There has been a sharp decline in membership due to increased withdrawals and a decrease in new recruits. Recent literature[4] gives a statistical picture of this breakdown in the United States.

- A recent National Opinion Research Center study indicated there is a larger relative number of resignees among those already established in church careers than in any other equivalent period of time since the French Revolution.

- For the years between 1965 and 1972, 66% of the yearly decrease in communities of religious women was due to dispensation or termination of vows. In communities of religious women the average annual net increase over these years was approximately 768 members, the average annual net decrease was 3,841—with only one-third of that loss caused by deaths.

- The total number of sisters in 1978 had declined 23% from 1960 and 29% since their peak membership year in 1966.

- The total number of religious brothers in 1978 had decreased 19% since 1960 and 32.5% since their peak membership year in 1967.

The purposes of religious communities, once clear and widely understood, have become vague and meaningless to some in the midst of the modern crisis. The structures of authority and the process of communication and decision making within religious communities seem no longer to fit the needs of the individuals within the community or suit the evolving work of the communities.

The processes of formation to religious community have sometimes become disorganized and seem to lack purpose. These and other signs indicate that the last fifteen to twenty

---

[4] Carroll W. Trageson and Pat Holden, "Existence and Analysis of the 'Vocation Crisis' in Religious Careers," in Carroll W. Trageson, John P. Koval, and Willis E. Bartlett, eds., *Report on Study of Church Vocations* (Notre Dame: Center for the Study of Man in Contemporary Society, 1974), pp. 1-3.

years have been a time when most religious communities have begun to experience breakdown. This cluster of the signs of breakdown in virtually all communities seems to indicate that we are approaching the end of another major era in the history of religious life.

Signs of Transition in Secular Culture

Church historians of the future will probably see the five centuries from about the year 1500 to the present as a unit forming a major cycle or episode. This unity stems from the fact that the rise and fall of the Modern Era in secular culture directly affected Church history. An illustration of this unity is a comparison of the doctrines on religious life proposed at Trent and Vatican II. At the start of the Modern Era the Council Fathers of Trent promulgated the teaching that the state of consecrated virginity was inherently better and holier than the married state. At the end of the Modern Era the Council Fathers at Vatican II taught that the religious life was no more a state of perfection than the Christian life in general. While the reconciliation of these seemingly contrary pronouncements remains still to be fully explained by professional theologians, the move away from the Tridentine theory of religious life is typical of all the ways in which Vatican II proclaimed that the Church had come to the end of the Modern Era. The Counter-Reformation is over and ecumenism has begun. In principle the Council Fathers at Vatican II have declared that there will be a *rapprochement* with the non-Christian religions and that the secular world is no longer the enemy. This shift away from directions the Church had followed throughout the Modern Era has been precipitated by the fact that secular culture as a whole is coming to the end of the Modern Era. While it is not possible to foretell what the coming age of religious life will look like in all details, it is possible to point out those features of present-day religious life which will not be there in the future precisely because they are the result of Modern assumptions absorbed into religious life during the last five hundred years.

The shape of the coming era of secular history will affect the coming age of religious life. Commentators have suggested that the post-Modern Era will be at least post-Christian, post-humanist, post-industrial, post-competitive, and post-materialist. To the extent that any or all of these characteristics have up until now been absorbed by religious life, they will pass away as they fade in society as a whole. For example, if the use of institutions by nineteenth- and twentieth-century religious is a reflection of the assumptions underlying the industrial efficiency through modern mass production and the erection of plants where modern institutions can function efficiently, to that extent the use of institutions by religious will change in the post-industrial era. Institutions will surely be present in the apostolate of religious in the coming age, but they will not be valued for the same reasons they were valued in the Modern Era. If competition and materialism will disappear in the post-Modern Era, so will the present form of struggle between capitalism and communism. In this event religious will no longer seek to serve the masses oppressed by industrial civilization. They will probably seek to serve the oppressed but not in the ways of the nineteenth century. In general, the coming age of religious life will differ from that of the past at least by shedding those external characteristics it took on to be adapted to the Modern Era.

All in all, the religious of today have a long and toilsome road ahead of them. If the conjecture of this book is true, none of them will escape the old Chinese curse, "May you live in a time of transition." They need not despair, of course. A glance across history makes it seem reasonable that religious life will last as long as the Church. It has shown a remarkable staying power despite its many ups and downs. On the other hand, it will probably be a good while yet before the main features of the next era in the history of religious life begin to emerge in easily discernible form. Hopefully, the ideas assembled in this chapter throw some light on the activities and frustrations, the dreams and disappointments, and the joys and sorrows that will fill the intervening years.

Chapter Two

The Life Cycle of a Religious Community: *A Sociological Model*

THE PREVIOUS CHAPTER FOCUSED ON A HISTORICAL MODEL FOR the evolution of religious life as such within the Church; in this chapter attention is turned toward the life of the individual religious community or institute. To this end, a sociological model for the life cycle of individual religious communities which organizes the important dimensions of each period in the life of the communities is developed.[1] This model allows further probing of the questions concerning the plausibility of a revitalization of religious life, since revitalization of present religious communities is one way that religious life as a whole will be renewed.

Organizing Concepts

To date, only thirteen men's religious orders in the entire history of the Church have ever surpassed a membership figure of 10,000 at some point in their existence. The mem-

---

[1] Some sources used to clarify the notion of a life cycle were: Hostie, *Vie et mort*; Wallace, "Paradigmatic Processes"; Gordon L. Lippitt and Warren H. Schmidt, "Crisis in a Developing Organization," *Harvard Business Review* 45 (November/December 1967) 102-12; Lawrence E. Greiner, "Evolution and Revolution as Organizations Grow," *Harvard Business Review* 50 (July/August 1972) 37-46; Thomas F. O'Dea, *The Sociology of Religion* (Englewood Cliffs, N.J.: Prentice-Hall, 1966); and Luther P. Gerlach and Virginia H. Hine, *People, Power and Change: Movements of Social Transformation* (Indianapolis: Bobbs-Merrill, 1970).

bership pattern of three of these orders—the Dominicans, the Minims, and the Jesuits—is graphed in Figure 2.1. Although these three examples are taken from among the largest orders of the Church, they are representative of the membership pattern in most religious communities, large or small. Typically one finds one or more cycles of growth and decline in the number of members.

These membership patterns suggest a dynamic inner vitality that goes on in a religious community. Using such analogies as the human life cycle and other cycles of growth and decline, a sociological model has been devised which divides the life cycle of an active religious community into five periods: foundation, expansion, stabilization, breakdown, and critical. The model is shown schematically in Figure 2.2. The shape of this curve is intended to represent the overall vitality of the community as it passes from one period to the next. In the following section salient events and characteristics which typify each of these periods are described. An attempt is also made to isolate the crises which occur during each period.

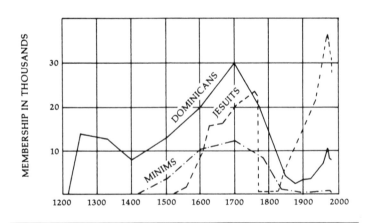

FIGURE 2.1: Membership of Dominicans, Minims, and Jesuits

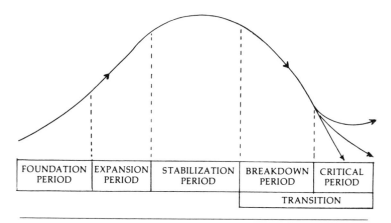

FOUNDATION PERIOD	EXPANSION PERIOD	STABILIZATION PERIOD	BREAKDOWN PERIOD	CRITICAL PERIOD
			TRANSITION	

FIGURE 2.2: Life Cycle of a Religious Community

The Periods of the Life Cycle

1. *The Foundation Period*

The first period in the life of a religious community centers around a founding person and his or her vision. The founder or foundress undergoes a radically transforming experience, which can usually be pinpointed to an event or series of events, and which is perceived as an abrupt shift in the founding person's identity and a timeless moment in which a vision or dream is received. Contained in the transforming experience is a new appreciation of the message of Jesus which leads to innovative insight concerning how the condition of the Church or society could be dramatically improved or how a totally new kind of future could be launched. A new impetus to live the religious life in all the totality of its demands is felt, and a new theory emerges that is at once a critique of the present, an appropriation of the past, a compelling image of the future, and a basis for novel strategies.

The founding person's transforming experience is followed by the initial emergence of the community. A fortuitous encounter takes place between the founder or foundress and some contemporary men or women in which the founding experience, innovative insight, emerging theory, and call to holiness are shared. The group unites under the guidance of the founding person to search for and invent new arrangements for living the gospel together and working toward the realization of the Kingdom of God.

The foundation period may last ten to twenty years or longer, and frequently coincides with the last part of the founding person's lifetime. Integration and cohesion center on the founding person and still more deeply on the person of Christ. The structural identity of the community appears in seminal form, and authority in the community springs from the wisdom of the founding person.

Founding events of religious communities have a uniqueness about them which has caused them to be especially treasured as significant moments in the Church's past. Examples of founding persons and their visions readily come to mind: Angela Merici's dream of a new kind of religious life for women that centered on an active apostolate; the hopes of Robert of Molesme to restore fervor through the strict observance of Benedict's *Rule* in the wilderness of Cîteaux; Don Bosco's contagious vision of loving Christ and joyfully serving the poor. The more striking cases of founding persons receiving their inspirations have become a part of the common heritage of all religious: Antony hearing in a Sunday gospel the words which were the key to his life's aim; Ignatius retiring to Manresa to receive his vision.

For the most part the foundation period is a time of grace and charism for a new religious community. But there are also crises that must be faced. The crisis of direction forces the community to decide which undertakings are important and which must be sacrificed. The crisis of leadership confronts the community with the problem of finding out how it will live beyond the time of its founding person. The crisis of legitimization involves the nascent community with the question of whether or not the Church will approve it as an authentic form of religious life. The Waldensians, for example, showed some signs of becoming a new religious order on the pattern of the mendicants, but they never overcame the crisis of legitimization. Instead of becoming a religious community, they ended up as renegades who had to hide out in the woods of medieval Europe.

2. The Expansion Period

When the community has emerged from the foundation period, it undergoes a fairly long period of expansion, during which the founding charism is institutionalized in a variety of ways. A community cult and belief system solidify, a community polity is fashioned, and community norms and customs take hold.

As members of the community's second generation mature and grow older, they recount stories of the foundation, which they have heard from the pioneers or have themselves experienced in their youth. These stories enshrine decisive events which set the community's direction or establish its characteristic traits. Gradually, rituals and symbols which express and commemorate the most treasured facets of the foundation are fused with the lore of the older members into a sort of sacred memory and cult that begins to be passed on from generation to generation as the community's "founding myth."

Attempts are made at thinking through the founding myth and expressing it in terms of contemporary thought patterns. Eventually these efforts result in theories, interpretations, and social models which coalesce into a belief system and give a rational structure to the more intuitive thrust of the founding myth.

Simultaneously, procedures are devised for community decision making and communication, and bit by bit the community's polity takes shape. Norms are set down and customs emerge which cover all aspects of the community's life, such as membership criteria, leadership standards, and apostolic priorities.

The members of the young community experience an excitement about the growth and success that characterize the expansion period. Large numbers join the community, and new works are rapidly taken on which enhance the possibility of a still broader recruitment. Major interpreters of the founding vision are recognized. Patterns of spiritual practice are determined, and the community's spirituality is made concrete in manuals of direction or other written documents.

With expansion come certain organizational crises. How is authority to be delegated? What means will be used to integrate and tie together the rapidly expanding network of establishments and the burgeoning membership? When Bernard joined the Cistercians thirteen years after their foundation, he led the community through this kind of organizational crisis. In the process, a new entity, the general chapter, was invented to cope with the situation, and this innovation is still a standard feature of most religious orders today. Another crisis of this period centers on maintaining the pristine vigor of the founding vision. As rival interpretations arise, which will be discarded? A classic example of this kind of crisis occurred in the great debates about poverty among the early Franciscans just after Francis died.

3. The Stabilization Period

After a fairly long expansion, which may last two to three generations or longer, there ensues a period of stabilization. Numerical increase in membership may continue, but geographical expansion usually slows down. The stabilization period may last a century or more, but is sometimes as brief as fifty years.

A feeling of success pervades the community during the stabilization period. Members experience a high degree of personal satisfaction from simply being in the community. The prevailing image of religious life is clear and accepted. It provides a basis for describing unambiguous social roles for religious. The community is accomplishing its purpose and this purpose is self-evident. The need to improve is not seen as a need to change things but simply to do better what is already being done. Gradually, as stabilization sets in, more and more of the community assumes that religious life has always been the way it is now and that it will always remain so in the future. There is little need to elaborate the understanding of the founding vision or penetrate into it more deeply. It is simply accepted, and repeated to new members. No one is left in the community who knew the founding person or the first disciples personally. Memory of the founding events takes on the cast of past history that is separate from the present moment. Formation of new members emphasizes their conformity to standard patterns of external behavior that are seen as the best means of cultivating interior commitment. The overall feeling of success which is so typical of the stabilization period is not illusory. There is, in fact, a job that is being done and done well by the many generous religious who devote themselves to its accomplishment.

The kinds of crises that crop up during the stabilization period are linked to the other characteristics of the period. The crisis of activism occurs. Members become so absorbed in work that they lose sight of its spiritual and apostolic underpinning. They allow the satisfactions of accomplishment to displace a centeredness in Christ. There is a loss of intensity of vision and commitment among members, now that the community has become so highly institutionalized. They can often be simply carried along by the sheer momentum of the community's activity and held in place by the pressure of social expectation placed on their role as religious by people in the Church. Another danger stems from the crisis of adaptation. In the midst of success the community is seldom open to adaptation, and any changes that have to be made are fraught with difficulty. Quite often, even the most legitimate changes are rejected, and their proponents are righteously and intolerantly silenced. The failure of later Jesuit missionaries to implement the ideas of Matteo Ricci concerning Confucian practices among Chinese Catholics is perhaps a good example of the sort of resistance to adaptation that can be found during the stabilization period.

4. *The Breakdown Period*

Eventually the seeming immutabilities of the stabilization period start to give, and the religious community enters the breakdown period. The breakdown may be gradual and last half a century or more, or it may be rapid and run its course in a few decades. In either case, what happens is a dismantling of the institutional structures and belief systems that arose in the expansion period and served the community so well during the stabilization period. This collective decline gives rise, in turn, to stress and doubt in the individual members.

Initially a number of persons become dissatisfied with the current state of the community. Perhaps they are simply struck by what they judge to be the silliness of some of the community's customs or procedures. Or they may come to see that the community's life and work are not equipped to handle important new challenges. Unanswered questions about the function and purpose of the community begin to accumulate and raise doubts. Levels of individual stress increase slowly at the beginning, but then rise rapidly as doubt spreads to more and more levels of the community's social structure.

To handle the growing problems, standard remedies are tried. All that is needed, it seems, is to get back to doing well what has always been done and to renew commitment to the community's mission. However, the usual problem-solving techniques become increasingly ineffective. A sense of crisis grows as community authority and decision-making structures become confused. The community's belief system begins to appear archaic and bound in by the trappings and articulations of a bygone age. The founding experience and myth, which had been internalized by the community's early generations, is no longer felt by the members.

As the community loses its sense of identity and purpose, service to the Church becomes haphazard and lacks direction. Moral norms in the community are relaxed and some members perhaps distract themselves with sex and misuse of wealth. There is a net loss of membership through increased withdrawals and decreased recruitment of new members.

The crises that arise during the breakdown period center on the various phenomena of decline in the community. The crisis of polarization can become acute when those who have faith in the community as it was align themselves against those who in varying degrees reject the community as it is. The crisis of collapsing institutions sets in as the community is forced to stop doing "business as usual" and abandon long-established works. The resulting demoralization leads to the crisis of the community's impending death. What is to be done as the chilling awareness grows in the community that it is inexorably listing into disintegration?

5. *The Critical Period*

The breakdown is followed by the critical period. Three outcomes are possible for religious communities during this period: extinction, minimal survival, or revitalization.

Extinction occurs when all the members of a community either withdraw or die and it simply passes out of existence. This happened, for example, to 76% of all men's religious orders founded before 1500 and to 64% of those founded before 1800. From a historical perspective, then, a reasonable expectation would seem to be that most religious communities in the Church today will eventually become extinct.

A religious community which does not die out may go into a long period of low-level or minimal survival. If the membership pattern of presently existing religious orders founded before the French Revolution is examined, one finds that most of them enter into a period lasting across several centuries in which the number of members is very low. In fact, only 5% of all men's orders founded before 1500 and only 11% of the orders founded before 1800 have a current membership which is larger than 2,000. The Minims (Figure 2.1) are typical of the orders which once were quite large and now have a small membership. This type of outcome should not be interpreted as a disappearance of vitality in every case. The Carthusians, too, follow this membership pattern. Yet they seem to be living up to their reputation of never having relaxed their observance—never reformed and never needing reform. To this day the order's spiritual impact appears greater than its numerical strength.

There is also a small percentage of religious communities which survive the critical period and enter into a period of revitalization. At least three characteristics can be singled out in all communities which have been revitalized in this way: a transforming response to the signs of the times; a reappropriation of the founding charism; and a profound renewal of the life of prayer, faith, and centeredness in Christ.

The time in history in which revitalization occurs seems to make a difference. If the revitalization occurs during one of the shifts in the dominant image of religious life singled out in the historical model (see Chapter One), the community takes on many of the characteristics of the emerging image, and a transforming response to the signs of the times seems central to the revitalization. If the revitalization occurs midway in one of the major eras in the history of religious life identified earlier, the revitalization takes on the characteristics of a reform, with the reappropriation of the founding charism playing a central role.

In either case, the community experiences the revitalization as a second foundation. Personal transformation or conversion is central to revitalization. With personal transformation comes innovative insight and a new centering in the person of Christ. The innovative insight allows the transformed individuals within the community to develop critical awareness of the assumptions underlying the traditional meaning of the community and the functioning of that community within the Church and the world. This innovative insight brings with it a focusing of energies through a new positive vision of what the community should be in the future. The vision allows the emergence of a new theory which gives meaning to the experiences of individuals and the shared events lived within the community, and spurs the community to building and creating its future. Such a new theory guides the community in the search for and the invention of new models of living together as a community bound by the evangelic conditions of discipleship in the service of the Church.

To further examine the sociological model of the life cycle of a religious community that has just been proposed, it will be used in the next section of this chapter to survey the history of the Ursulines. This example will serve as a test case to estimate the model's utility and applicability and to assay its advantages and limitations as a tool for interpreting the history of a specific religious order or congregation.

Ursuline Example

Two cycles of the type envisioned in the sociological model can be distinguished in the history of the Ursulines to date.

First Cycle

1535-1565	Foundation	30 years
1565-1690	Expansion	125 years
1690-1790	Stabilization	100 years
1790-1820	Breakdown	30 years
		285 years

Second Cycle

1820-1840	Revitalization	20 years
1840-1900	Expansion	60 years
1900-1960	Stabilization	60 years
1960-	Breakdown	18+ years
		158+ years

The transition (which includes the critical period) linking these two cycles lasted fifty years, from the start of the first breakdown in 1790 to the end of the nineteenth-century revitalization in 1840. Although the second cycle has not yet run its course, it seems that a second transition has been under way for about two decades now. If the time span of the first transition is used to extrapolate into the next cycle of the model, another revitalization should become recognizable around 1990 and should finally issue in a third expansion period sometime around 2010. Whether such an extrapolation is warranted depends, of course, on whether the neat

symmetries in the above-proposed division of years corre-
spond at all to the actual rhythms of Ursuline life during the
last four and a half centuries.

The Foundress

Angela Merici founded the Company of Saint Ursula in 1535,
five years before she died. Viewed in retrospect, her whole
life turned out to be a rather apt preparation for founding the
order. Born in 1474, or perhaps a few years earlier, in Desen-
zano, a small town midway between Brescia and Verona
along the Milan-Venice highroad, she lived in northern Italy
while it still led the rest of Europe in economic and cultural
dominance. There is less than a decade's difference between
Angela's lifespan and that of Michelangelo, Machiavelli,
Raphael, and Caesar and Lucretia Borgia, the offspring of
Alexander VI. Outside Italy, this list of Angela's immediate
contemporaries includes Copernicus, Erasmus, Thomas
More, and Luther. During her lifetime Columbus discovered
America, Lorenzo the Magnificent brought the Florentine Renaissance to its peak, Savanarola was burned at the stake,
Leonardo da Vinci painted the *Mona Lisa,* and Henry VIII rid
himself of three wives. Angela's generation witnessed one of
the great turning points in Western civilization.

If the sixteenth-century reform within the Catholic Church
is divided into the "gentle" reform preceding the Council of
Trent (1545-63) and the "rigorous" reform following it,
Angela emerges as a typical figure and one of the best examples of the earlier reform. For as long as anyone could remember there had been endless talk of reform, but in the
early decades of the new century the optimistic perspectives
of the Renaissance made at least some people think that some
sort of reform would be realized after all. No one yet anticipated the bitterness of the divisions that would result later in
the century from the questions Luther was then raising north
of the Alps. In Italy, small groups of lay people together with
a band of zealous clergy were experimenting with various
programs to regenerate the Church. Carafa (the future Paul
IV) and Gaetano with the Theatines, Emiliani with the

Somascinians, and Zaccaria with the Barnabites were devising a new style of priestly life aimed at sincere personal holiness in the midst of active pastoral service. The Jesuits would later adopt and perfect this priestly lifestyle, that of the clerics regular, and show it to be the most successful innovation of men's religious life in the Modern Era. It was also during the early decades of the century that Carafa helped Bascio and Fossombrone launch the Capuchin reform of the Franciscans.

Angela was familiar with many of these efforts, but she was closely involved with another project in which Carafa was then participating: the Divine Love Movement, a network of small and fervent communities of lay people and priests in the main cities of Italy. The Movement operated centers to shelter orphans and pilgrims and to care for the sick, especially the "incurables," victims of the first epidemic of syphilis sweeping across Europe at this time. Besides operating these centers, Movement members gathered to pray together and to share ideas on renewing the Church. Among the persons in the Divine Love communities were scions of noble families, leading intellectuals, wealthy patrons of the arts, influential theologians, progressive prelates, and highly placed members of the Curia. Angela had a pleasant, outgoing personality and a secure sense of personal worth, and she had no difficulty mixing with the more imposing members of the Divine Love Movement. She shared their concern for the Church and favored the positive and pragmatic approaches to reform that were being tried by the forward-looking members. To her informed awareness of the times she added a deep love and attachment to Christ. For the most part her piety was rather unobtrusive in comparison to some of the more public and emotional manifestations of the faith that were then in vogue. However, she enjoyed travel and made many pilgrimages to various Italian shrines; once, she even submitted to the rigors of the long and arduous trip to the Holy Land. As she matured she came to be seen as a prudent, wise, and holy spiritual guide; and many prominent personages, both lay and ecclesiastic, came to ask her advice and receive her kind but sensible direction.

Foundation Period

Angela remained single during these years of association with the early Italian reformers. She was well acquainted with women's religious life, of course, but the kind of concern for the Church's welfare in which Angela was involved was not found in the cloistered convents of her day. Angela never became a religious. She was quite content with being a Franciscan tertiary and taking seriously the obligations of this engagement. On a still deeper level, her life had been marked by a singular event that occurred when she was in her early thirties. In 1506 she had a vision of a comely woman clothed in a full cape. Slowly, this woman, whom Angela recognized as Saint Ursula, spread apart the sides of the wide cape to reveal a long advancing procession of maidens accompanied by angels and trailing back far into the distance. Angela understood this vision to mean that one day before she died she would found a company of virgins dedicated to Ursula and committed to serving Christ down through the ages. Angela interpreted the vision as a gift from God and willingly embraced its meaning. Although the rest of her life received an inner direction from this transforming event, she told few people about it. She was not given to joining the enthusiastic commotion that surrounded reputed apparitions in her day. Instead she quietly gave herself to a steadily deepening relationship with Christ, confident that when the time was right the foretold event would take place.

More than twenty-five years passed. Angela was living in Brescia, next door to Saint Afra's Church, when she came into contact with the women who would comprise the new group. Angela was helping them undertake various good works similar to those of the Divine Love communities. The young women were also engaged in giving catechetical lessons to the children of Brescia in the manner of the new Christian Doctrine Movement which sought to renew the Church by teaching youth the simple truths of their faith. During the course of the year 1535, she invited several of the women to unite into a group to mutually support one another in their own commitment to Christ and to strengthen and perpetuate the works in which they were engaged. The actual foundation was quite simple. On November 25, after going to mass and communion together at St. Afra's, twenty-eight young women met with Angela in the sacristy. They agreed that the Company of Saint Ursula was begun and begged God's blessing on the new undertaking. The group was unlike any form of women's religious life of that time. The women lived with their families, agreed to remain unmarried for the sake of the gospel, continued the various works in which they were already engaged, and met with Angela singly or in groups to deepen their understanding of the commitment they had made and to deepen their generosity to live it more fully.

The little group was a lay community in composition, spirituality, and basic direction, distinct from the monastic and religious life of the day and not related to the official clergy by any special relationship. Later, of course, the Church would expand its notion of women's religious life and the Ursulines would adapt in various ways to become classified as religious in the technical sense. However, at the start, Angela was not concerned with conforming the nascent group to the regnant definition of religious life, especially since the apostolic service which was at the very heart of the group's spirit would have been impossible had the group adopted the form of cloister then required of all women religious. Another distinguishing feature lay in the fact that the new group was clearly a women's affair right from the start. Angela is the first major foundress of an exclusively women's community. (Both Brigits, of Ireland and of Sweden, founded double monasteries.) There was never a male counterpart to the Ursulines nor the intention of one. Angela saw new possibilities for women. She knew from experience that a group of women could commit itself to the "active life" of apostolic service within the larger Christian community without habit or cloister, all the while remaining celibate in such "secular" circumstances. For more than a century, the social structure of European cities had already opened the possibility of a somewhat similar lifestyle for women in groups such as the Beguines. But the Beguines usually worked together with the Beghards and were often suspect of not living up to the virtue they professed. Angela's Ursulines did not have this difficulty.

An atmosphere of friendly charity and honest joy permeated the rapidly growing company. There were one hundred and fifty members in 1540, when the sad news that Angela was on her deathbed spread through the community. She had given them a short and practical rule describing their way of life together with a series of final testaments. Among them is the testament of adaptability: Should the passing of time or other circumstances require new regulations or adaptations of any kind of your way of doing things, make the changes carefully and with the help of wise counsel. In the coming years Ursulines would follow this advice in a variety of ways. Angela encouraged them to proceed into the future with hope, promising them that even after her death she would always be with them in spirit. She died happily, surrounded by her sisters.

The remaining years of the foundation period did not pass without troubles. Five years after Angela died, the Institute was shaken by attempts to "protect" the virgins by a wall (cloister) or, since they resisted this, by some distinctive habit. The issue of the habit became a bone of contention among the sisters. The compromise they finally worked out was to dress in black and wear the leather belts which have endured as a well-known and distinctive Ursuline feature down to the present century.

Expansion in Italy and France

The expansion period of the first great cycle of Ursuline history occurred in two phases: expansion to Milan and the rest of northern Italy under the influence of Charles Borromeo beginning in 1565, and expansion into France under the leadership of Frances de Bermond beginning in 1596.

Shortly after the close of the Council of Trent, Borromeo, one of the Council's main leaders and Milan's gifted archbishop, called the Ursulines to his city. The catechetical methods of the Christian Doctrine Movement had been strongly endorsed by Trent, and Borromeo lent his organizing genius to perfecting this work in Milan and its suffragan dioceses. He had found out about the Ursulines' success with this work in Brescia, and he wanted them to take it up in Milan. In the process he promoted the Ursulines in many ways and guided their growth. The prestige of Borromeo's reputation and his great satisfaction with the Ursulines led to their being called to dioceses all over Italy. Borromeo encouraged the Ursulines to live together in communities. He believed that life in common would enhance their spiritual and apostolic life and would besides be more in conformity with Trent's reemphasis of cloister, even though he knew the Ursulines were technically not religious. The Council had once more pronounced that cloister was of the very essence of women's religious life, and Pius V was at that time promulgating various measures throughout the universal Church that insisted on cloister being enforced for women religious with no exceptions. Gradually the modification of life in common became the norm for Italian Ursulines. In 1572, just after the death of Pius V, the Institute of Angela Merici received papal confirmation from Gregory XIII in this "conventualized" (but not cloistered) pattern that Borromeo had recommended.

The French expansion centers around the person of Frances de Bermond, a noblewoman from the south of France who had been engaged in charitable works not unlike those of the Ursulines. In 1596 she became acquainted with the Borromean version of Angela's rule, and she decided to dedicate her life to establishing the Ursulines in France. During the closing years of the 1500s and the first two decades of the 1600s, Mother de Bermond founded many communities. Of all these foundations, the one in Paris was probably the most auspicious.

At this time the cultural, economic, and political leadership of Europe was passing over from Italy and Spain to France, where it would be perfected by Richelieu and reach its zenith during the reign of Louis XIV. The first half of the seventeenth century was also the golden age of the masters of the French School of spirituality—Bérulle, Olier, Vincent de Paul, and their disciples—and Paris was the focus of this blossoming. Hence, when two Parisian noblewomen, Madame Acarie and Madame de Sainte Beuve, in consultation with Cardinal Bérulle, invited Mother de Bermond to Paris to help them start an Ursuline establishment, the seeds were sown for plentiful future harvests. Just as in the case of Borromeo, this situation caused some significant modifications in Ursuline life. Madame de Sainte Beuve, a persuasive and forceful woman, was convinced that nothing less than the Tridentine ideal of women's religious life should characterize the Ursulines in Paris and, furthermore, that the Paris Ursulines would be true nuns in the full technical sense of the word. These aims required cloister and the adoption of one of the ancient rules of the only officially recognized orders of the Church. The Paris Ursulines chose the Rule of Saint Augustine, whose reputation was then on the ascendancy in Paris, and professed solemn vows according to the terms laid down in that Rule. Madame de Sainte Beuve became the first superior. The enclosure of the new foundation was mitigated to allow young girls to enter the cloister area where the convent school was located. This accommodation to the Ursuline apostolate was reinforced by the addition of a fourth vow of instruction, another special feature of the Paris Ursulines. Within the cloister the nuns wore an impeccably designed habit. All these changes were given special papal approval, obtained at the behest of influential friends of Madame de Sainte Beuve.

The new house with its convent school enjoyed a widely acclaimed success in the French capital. Soon daughter houses following the same special provisions of the Paris Ursulines were springing up in France and other regions within the orbit of French influence, and taken together these houses made up the Paris Congregation of the Ursulines. While the Paris Ursulines did not neglect serving the poor, their schools rapidly grew in prestige and became the elite convent schools of French society. In 1639 a small group of nuns from the Paris Congregation led by Mother Marie of the Incarnation founded a convent in Québec, the chief settlement of French Canada. In many ways the intrepid Marie of the Incarnation resembled Angela. Marie was an active, practical woman who thrived on creating a new apostolate among the Indians of New France; at the same time she was profoundly contemplative with a mystical attachment to Christ.

Another important grouping of Ursuline houses made up the Bordeaux Congregation, comprising the houses stemming from Mother de Bermond's foundation in that city. By the end of the expansion period, there were about 9,000 French Ursulines in some 350 houses. (By way of comparison, there are presently about 21,000 Ursulines worldwide, counting all the branches.) In the course of the expansion period several major variations of Angela's inspiration had developed in response to the various needs and aspirations of the times. These variations reflected the chief characteristics of religious life during the period when the Church and European culture entered the Modern Era.

Stabilization and Transition

The eighteenth century was a stabilization period for the Ursulines. The main concentrations were in Italy, France, and Catholic Germany. There were a few new foundations during the century. The celebrated New Orleans convent, for example, was founded in 1727. However, there were no large-scale expansions to new regions. The lifestyles and teaching methods fashioned during the expansion period were continued and refined, but not substantially changed. In contrast to the relaxed spirit and mild, enlightened decadence that spread through men's religious life, the Ursulines' level of fervor remained exemplary throughout the course of the eighteenth century. On the eve of the French Revolution, the condition of the Ursulines worldwide was satisfactory and in many ways quite successful; they had come a long way from the humble beginnings in Brescia a century and a half earlier.

In the meanwhile, the powerful forces of history relentlessly moved forward. Along with the other orders that made up the vast complex of religious life at the end of the century, the Ursulines suffered the violent plundering and government confiscation of houses, property, and goods which marked the onset of the breakdown period. This spoliation started in France with the Reign of Terror, and within a period of thirty years had extended to Italy, Germany, and the rest of Catholic Europe. In the vast majority of Ursuline convents, the religious were dispersed. Resistance was futile and often dangerous; in fact, it led to martyrdom for the Ursulines of Valenciennes in 1794. In a few short years, the work that had taken so long to be painstakingly built up and maintained was virtually destroyed. However, in 1807, in the very midst of these darkest hours of Ursuline history, Angela was canonized. Although her scattered followers across the world could not adequately celebrate this honor given their foundress, they could draw hope from what was perhaps a providential sign for the future.

The critical period in Ursuline history lasted the brief twenty years from 1820 to 1840. It is known today that the period was a true revitalization and second foundation, but this fact was not at all clear to the Ursulines who lived through it. Napoleon had been overthrown in 1815, and there was a break in the fury of antireligious sentiment. Here and there a handful of Ursuline houses were left in places off the beaten track. The communities in these houses that had weathered the storm were old and diminished in numbers due to the long years in which recruitment had been interrupted. A few "ex-Ursulines," who were "living in the world" and by then advanced in age, managed to buy back some old Ursuline convents in order to reopen them as religious houses. Thus, slowly, they set themselves to the task of restoring at least a part of what had existed before. These women had no way of knowing if they would succeed. By almost any human estimate, their prospects were dim indeed. There was no way of reopening all the houses that had once been in existence. The old sisters who could remember knew that these humble efforts were a far cry from the large, efficiently organized, and productive network of Ursuline houses of the past. The young newcomers would lend only their generosity to the work. Gradually, the Catholic revival of the early nineteenth century helped these Ursuline second beginnings. So many things in the Church and society had changed that it was impossible to reproduce all the features of the previous era. But it was also known that many variations of the Ursuline inspiration had worked in the past, especially because of the expanded knowledge of Ursuline history and Angela's original project that followed the canonization process. The testament of adaptability that Angela had included in the heritage of recommendations she expressly left for her sisters had, in fact, been heeded. Perhaps this facet of the Ursuline charism would again allow for changes in the "way of doing things" required by "the passing of time or other circumstances." The overall awareness of Angela's thought and spirit among Ursulines has probably been much more explicit during the second cycle of their history (i.e., since the revitalization of 1820-40) than during the first. Similarly, the figure and person of Angela has probably been much more a source of inspiration, edification, and pride for Ursulines during the last one hundred and fifty years.

Second Cycle

The second expansion period lasted sixty years. By mid-century a pattern of recruitment and growth had begun in the reestablished houses of Italy, France, and Germany, the regions that had been hardest hit by the secularizations. Some of these houses were strong enough to respond to appeals of North American bishops for help in serving their flocks, then rapidly expanding with the influx of Catholic immigrants from Europe. In this manner, the existing Ursuline houses of North America were augmented by a string of new foundations, such as those of Brown County, Ohio, in 1845, Cleveland in 1850, Louisville in 1853, and Chatham, Ontario, in 1860. In countries undergoing nineteenth-century industrialization and then in other parts of the world, Ursulines lent their energy to the Church's efforts to cope with the challenges of the times by shoring up the pastoral ministry with schools and hospitals.

Many variations of the flexible Ursuline charism had appeared during the course of the first expansion, ranging from Angela's Brescian community (something like a present-day secular institute) to Madame de Sainte Beuve's Parisian convent (an order according to the official seventeenth-century definition of the term). The same process repeated itself during the second expansion. Some Ursulines were cloistered, others were not. Some professed solemn vows, others professed simple vows according to the formula the Vatican was then devising for the new-style congregations. Some preserved the distinction between choir nuns and lay sisters, others devised forms of egalitarian communities. Some served the poor, others the rich. Some worked under the pioneering conditions of the United States frontier, others carried on the traditions of serving the genteel noblesse begun by the former Paris Congregation. Some belonged to single autonomous houses, others moved among the many houses of large international congregations. Some were "religious" according to the Vatican's nineteenth-century definition, others were not.

An event which can be used to signal the start of the second stabilization is the effort of Leo XIII to bring some order into the rich profusion of Ursuline variety that had flowered during the second expansion. At the turn of the century he invited the Ursulines of the world to unite into one large organization, centered in Rome. About two-thirds decided to do so and formed the Roman Union, which provided many organizational advantages in the following decades. With the publication of the *Normae* of 1901, all Ursulines were finally recognized as religious by the Vatican. In the twentieth century the vast Ursuline family has served the Church generously and effectively, realizing the ideals common to all religious during the Age of the Teaching Congregations, and at the same time embodying the charism of apostolic holiness that appeared for the first time with Angela and her sisters in Brescia.

At present, the external signs of breakdown have once again appeared. Together with other religious, Ursulines across the world have entered a time of decreasing statistics. It is still too early to assess fully the meaning of these trends. A century hence it will be possible to look back and see if they were just minor fluctuations in a long stabilization period or the first signs of an actual transition. Nevertheless, it is possible at this time to examine the consequences of the latter alternative considered as a tentative conjecture.

The falling statistical trends are averages, of course. Ursuline membership figures in some regions of Europe, for example, began to drop more than a decade before the worldwide statistics. On the other hand, there are a few places where membership has been modestly increasing all along. If this is the start of a breakdown period, it differs from the last one. There are now no large-scale secularizations of Ursuline communities or government seizure of their houses. While maintaining fairly well their standing commitments to serve the Church's presence in various institutions, Ursulines are also asking about the meaning of their presence in the larger Christian community. One finds Ursulines representing the range of attitudes in today's Church from the "liberal" to the "conservative." In the United States, it was a group of Ursulines who caused the first public stir in the news media about experimental habits resembling airline-stewardess uniforms. On the other hand, there were Ursulines involved in the discussion of the advisability of establishing the *Consortium Perfectae Caritatis*. On the larger international plane, one finds an excellent example of serious research into an order's founding charism with the Ursulines. Studies such as those of Teresa Ledochowska combine good historical scholarship with a loving effort to evoke the mind and heart of Angela and make her life and thought understandable and accessible to the present time. Angela is surely present with her sisters in spirit, as she promised to be, as they read the pages of these well-done works.

If one is a religious today, no matter what community one belongs to, it will be worthwhile to pay attention to the Ursulines. Will they once more find reason to heed Angela's testament of adaptability? If so, what changes will they make and who will they select as the "wise counsel" to help them make the changes? In the past they selected the likes of Borromeo and Bérulle. Who will it be this time? The answers to such questions as these will be instructive to all religious. But it is the Ursulines of this generation who will have the privilege of fashioning the coming episode of the Ursuline story and advancing into their third expansion period, should the conjecture here proposed turn out to be the case.

Some Limitations and Generalizations

Limitations

The models proposed for the evolution of religious life in Chapter One and for the life cycle of a religious community in this chapter are both simplifications. Some might validly question, for example, whether there were just five major eras in the history of religious life, and whether the transitions between the eras occurred as clearly as the historical model suggests. The description of the dominant image of religious life for each era is a simplification of what was in every case a rather complex phenomenon. Hopefully, the liberties that have been taken are justified by the intention of trying to synopsize the history of religious life in such a way as to make some tentative insights more easily accessible to someone who is not a professional historian.

Similarly, the breaks between the successive periods in the life cycle of a religious community are nowhere near as clear-cut as the proposed sociological model suggests. In history, breakdowns sometimes occur within one order in different geographical locales at different times. Revitalizations often occur in some places for an order while it decays elsewhere. At times there are orders in which the role of the founding person is rather minor and does not have the decisiveness described in the model. Some communities have been founded in rather modest historical circumstances that were not accompanied by the profound inspiration described in the model. These and similar qualifications must be kept in mind when the sociological model is used to interpret the life cycle of any particular community.

Generalizations

Some generalizations can be made about the sociological model. In the evolution of a religious community the nonrational elements of transforming experience, vision, and myth play a central role. This is especially true during the periods of foundation and revitalization. Although necessary for each period in the life cycle of a community, the techniques of rationality (long-range planning, leadership training, etc.) will never be sufficient to found a religious community or to revitalize one. The renewed vitality that comes to some religious communities during the time of transition finds its source in plumbing the depths of the mythic and nonrational and integrating them with the more rational dimensions of human life.

No individual community can remain unaffected by the larger historical pressures of the five ages sketched in the historical model. But seemingly small details make a big difference in giving each community its uniqueness. For example, if Angela had lived just fifty years later than she did, she still could have founded a religious order for women to meet the needs of the Age of the Apostolic Orders, but it probably would never have occurred to her to give her sisters the testament of adaptability. She would have been a contemporary of Pius V and, simply because she was such a responsive member of the Church, she may have phrased things with the granite-like, from-here-to-eternity type of terminology that Pius V had a habit of using. She probably would not have had the supple and pliable frame of mind of the "gentle" pre-Tridentine Catholic reform of the sixteenth century. Not just the century or age, but even the year of Angela's birth may have been providential for the eventual "inbreaking" of the Ursuline charism into history.

While it is true, as Santayana put it, that those who do not know history are often condemned to reliving it, it is also true that those who *do* know history are condemned to the same fate. One thing is sure: knowing history does not spare one the pains and joys of living through it. And while it is not yet feasible for all the religious in the world to gather for a mammoth planning session about what is to be done regarding the next turning point in the history of religious life, what is possible is to begin to take action in one's own congregation.

The sociological model is the springboard for concrete plans and actions for a religious institute that is part of a large, old family like the Franciscans or one that has started in this century like the Medical Missionaries of Mary. Knowing and understanding the major eras of religious life as outlined in Chapter Two is instructive and helpful, but it does not necessarily give one any handles on what to do here and now with the group of which one is a part. Chapter Three and the remaining chapters begin to provide ways and means for both the systematic and serendipitous.

However, a central insight of the myth of original sin is that humankind is not capable of sustained development; breakdown and disintegration are ever-recurring manifestations of the human condition. Since religious men and women exist within the human condition, it should not be surprising that, from time to time, all religious communities experience an extensive period of significant breakdown and disintegration. These bleak realities should be embraced with humble acceptance of the human condition and faith-filled hope that the Lord will in time resurrect life-giving initiatives from the death-dealing processes of breakdown.

Chapter Three

The Vitality Curve

EXPLORING THE HISTORICAL AND SOCIOLOGICAL MODELS OF Chapters One and Two is done neither as a purely intellectual exercise nor as mere museum dusting. Such exploration is done more purposefully: to discover the underlying pattern or design of historical, sociological movements in order to inform our present action and our planning for the future. Consequently, this chapter is important in that it articulates the possible meanings of this underlying pattern or design. Any model of community development that is true to a theme of this book, memory and hope, must build on what can be seen as a strong and consistent pattern in the life cycle of all human groups and the cyle, perhaps, of life itself. The Vitality Curve, to be described in this chapter, is such a model.

The Vitality Curve[1] (Figure 3.1) is a stylized slice of life, a conceptual framework for understanding "how life is." With it, it is possible to demonstrate the development and decline

---

[1] There are several traditions about the Vitality Curve. It was originally developed under the name "Provolution Grid," evolving out of the discussions of Robert Hoover, John Sherwood, and David Rumkorff which were aimed at understanding some of the reasons why conventional methodologies of social change have failed and, hopefully, to generate a new basis for understanding social change in all of its dimensions. In their investigations and discussions they did not limit themselves to the traditional behavioral and social sciences or to a modern "systems approach" but instead decided on an interdisciplinary approach which would include philosophy, history, and the study of religion. The theory of the Curve was first explained in the class notes that Robert Hoover wrote during the fall of 1969 when he was a professor of community planning at the University of Cincinnati. Since then the Curve has been further developed by David Rumkorff, John Sherwood, and Bruce Rodgers in their work at Management Design, Inc. (MDI), as well as by the authors of this book.

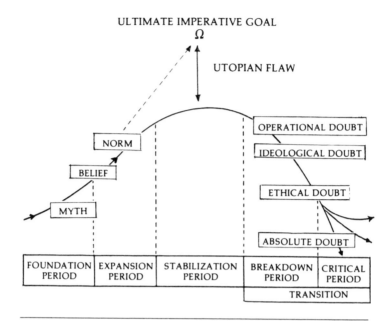

ULTIMATE IMPERATIVE GOAL
Ω

UTOPIAN FLAW

NORM

BELIEF

MYTH

OPERATIONAL DOUBT

IDEOLOGICAL DOUBT

ETHICAL DOUBT

ABSOLUTE DOUBT

FOUNDATION PERIOD	EXPANSION PERIOD	STABILIZATION PERIOD	BREAKDOWN PERIOD	CRITICAL PERIOD
			TRANSITION	

FIGURE 3.1: The Vitality Curve

of social reality. With it, it is possible to uncover the pattern of development and decline, and to learn from them.

Development Side

As we assumed in the Introduction, the revitalization of religious life is considered possible. In previous chapters a structure of evolution in religious life as well as individual congregations has been presented, indicating periods of growth, death, and rebirth. This first section of the exploration of the Vitality Curve will focus in a more detailed manner on the development side of the process, which can be called community development (see Figure 3.2).

A glance at the chart of the Curve (see Figure 3.1) reveals that three levels of social meaning form the underpinning for

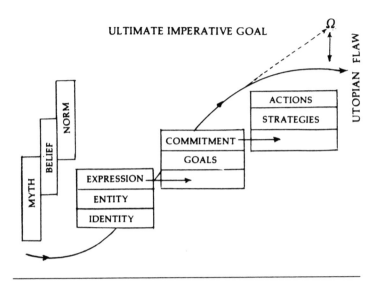

FIGURE 3.2: Development

the growth movements in religious life: myth, belief, norm. The community *myths* are the stories that capture the inner meaning of human life and constitute the paradigm for all of the significant actions of the community; they recount and celebrate how important dimensions of the community came into existence. The *beliefs* that emerge and coalesce as the community continues through time are the shared sets of understandings that members have about themselves, their relationships with other groups, and similar matters. These propositions about reality, which are accepted as true, reveal how the community appreciates or values the above dimensions of their life. They also function as a basis for choice, used to discriminate among the possibilities from which the group will select its activities. As a group develops so do *norms*, which are the stable patterns of expectations and actions in both the life and ministry aspects of community living. Community norms refer to the generally shared criteria used for judging individual and community action. The norms answer the continual question of the membership: "What do we do to effect the purposes of this community?"

The myths of a religious community should be understood as expressing the "really real" and not as a fairy tale.[2] These stories of what the founding persons or the first members did for the community reveal that they grappled with and came through a transforming experience with a sense of their own *identity*. Most often in this foundation period, the founders are graced with the charism of being able to articulate a vision which attracts more persons who are touched in their own depths; there begins the formation of a significant *entity*. In the normal dynamic of community development there subsequently arises the need and desire to *express* the communal vision in compelling, captivating images, ones which will continually evoke the ideal for the members. It is important to note that the response at the mythical level is nonrational. It is not *ir*rational; rather, it partakes of that mystery in the depths of the self that can never be understood entirely, yet which moves persons to do the most important things in their lives.

In the movement to the belief level of community development, the expression of the identity and entity becomes a means for the community to discover its goals. The beliefs act as antennae for the choices that must be made to effect the vision, and as such these understandings are held more on the rational level, though they are still alloyed with the nonrational. The tangible form that beliefs usually take is a book of constitutions, a rule, or a convenant.

The importance of beliefs in community development is evidenced when it is recalled that members of a religious community can think and act together only insofar as they can base their thoughts and actions on principles and data held in common, data with some degree of objectivity. If the

---

[2] See Louis Dupré, *The Other Dimension* (Garden City, N.Y.: Doubleday, 1972), chs. 4–6, for an excellent development of the role of myth in a community and for an important distinction between "demythologizing" and "demythizing."

group is to survive, or to flourish, the members need to carry on a continual conversation in terms of some basic heritage from a shared past. Normally it is through this conversation that consensus is reached about the future actions that the new signs of the times demand.

Hence, it is important to see how goals are related to the founding charism of a community. It is in the context of this charism that the choices inherent in *goal*-setting, besides generating an enthusiasm, will then indicate to what the community invites *commitment*. And without commitment, goals will remain words, never becoming results. Gaining commitment and participation in goal setting is a primary task that General or Provincial Councils must attend to, as they are especially charged with the responsibility of seeing that the "congregational conversation" includes pondering the *raison d'être* of the group.[3]

On the level of norms there are also three subcomponents. The "will to action" or the commitment that comes out of the beliefs of the community becomes a means to discover the *strategies* that must be devised, the nitty-gritty part of planning to build the Kingdom. What the framework of the Vitality Curve can do is remind us that for effectiveness at this point commitment is presumed. If something is not working well in the community, the Curve can be used as a diagnostic tool to find out where the problem is and wherein, perhaps, some intervention can be made. Again, the Curve reveals that strategizing is part of the whole fabric of the mission of the congregation. And while there are some members better at story telling than at strategizing and vice versa, using a conceptual scheme such as the Curve helps to keep everybody on board and using their particular gifts. It is in the strategies developed that a community is brought to the point of *action* that effects the results. It is not difficult to understand the many hours of meetings which must go into

---

[3] See Peter L. Berger and Thomas Luckmann, *The Social Construction of Reality* (Garden City, N.Y.: Doubleday, Anchor Books, 1976), pp. 152ff., for a discussion of conversation as "the most important vehicle of reality-maintenance."

TABLE 3.1: Examples of the Levels of Social Meaning

Levels of Social Meaning	Early Christian Community	Women's Movement	Afro-American Culture
Myth	Jesus	Matriarchy Eternal Woman	Black Power
Belief	"Blessed are the Pure of Heart" "Blessed are the Peacemakers"	"I Can do Anything" The Bonds of Sisterhood	"Black is Beautiful"
Norm	*Kerygma* *Koinonia* *Diakonia*	Talking back Equality	Black Capitalism

efforts to implement those actions coming out of the examples regarding norms given in the chart in Table 3.1. Believing that "blessed are the peacemakers" and effecting the kind of *diakonia* that makes peace require different gifts.

The development movement from myth to norm, from identity to action, leads to the term of the effort, or to what has been called the "ultimate imperative goal." This is the profound reality that motivates, calls one in the deepest part of the self. It is Martin Luther King's "I have a dream," or the peace movement's "Peace Now," or for the religious "the Kingdom of God." The ultimate imperative goal challenges the community myth, calls it up and renders it operative in one's life. The implications of the examples given reveal the communal dimension of the goal.

Some Implications of the Development Side
of the Vitality Curve

This section will briefly sketch some implications that could be drawn out from the development side of the Vitality

Curve. The development side is basically a movement of integration and cohesion. This is the essence of the service of administrators and formation personnel in religious communities. From this perspective, development can be seen as a process (or processes) of matching the myths, beliefs, and norms of the community with the individual's myths, beliefs, and norms. Both the community and the individual have charisms that must be respected and nurtured in this process; it is a movement toward organic wholeness.

If indeed the community myth is a paradigm which provides integration and social cohesion for the person and the group in the sense of ordering values, then it is important especially in initial formation phases that the program be shaped in such a way that individuals are moved to their depths. One of the elements in this movement might be some type of "desert experience" or a directed retreat. In some way the new member needs to resolve the "Who am I?" question through a felt resonance with the community myth. "Yahweh called me, before I was born, from my mother's womb he pronounced my name." With this experience the member can write his or her name under the myth.

Because both the individual and the community change over time, the symbols of expression of the myth of each often become time- and culture-bound. The symbols then too must change if they are to freight meaning over the long haul. This is often the service of directors of ongoing formation programs or of local superiors. Theological and scriptural updating, congregational heritage seminars, and an authentic working out of a mission for the local community are some ways that lead to a deepening understanding of the "really real" part of the myth of the congregation in such a way that each age and each member can continually express the truth of the charism of the congregation.

Perhaps a way to consider the implications of the belief level is through an example. Consider the railroad companies at the time of Kitty Hawk. Evidently their understanding of who they were could have been expressed: "We're railroaders!" Hence, the curious tinkerings of the Wright brothers and the event of Kitty Hawk were at best amusing. Imagine how differently they would have seen and responded to those events (and how much better off they would be now) had their understanding of themselves (beliefs) led them to the proposition: "We're in the *transportation* business!" With that kind of antenna and the money they had at their command, travellers probably would be calling the "American Transportation Company" for reservations instead of TWA or Amtrak.

Similarly, some religious orders that defined their mission as teaching or nursing are fast upon hard times as the traditional structures of Catholic schools and hospitals falter in the financial crisis. But to have expressed the mission as "education" or "health care" admits of searching out varied methods to fulfill the call. *Ora et labora* for the Benedictines and the Ignatian *Spiritual Exercises* are analogous types of understandings and processes that an order uses to choose among the many varieties of service and/or spirituality. General or Provincial Chapters, for example, must then continually work at discerning and discovering points of contact of the order's charism and the contemporary needs. And then follows the arduous task of translating that into a constitution or planning document, so that over time learning can be drawn from the exploration. This latter effort is perhaps one of the more challenging aspects of a "contemporary asceticism."

The social reality at the level of norms can be seen as a set of expectations. They tend to exert a prior influence on the exercise of freedom and the decisions of freedom in the community. For example, the image of the "good teacher" or the "good local superior" prevalent in a community will have a significant effect on novices or persons asked to serve in certain positions. If the development experience is not to be totally frustrating, individuals must be able to appropriate the prevailing image in a way that respects their own uniqueness as well as the needs of the congregation. Formation personnel aid this process by helping the members understand and accept both the glories and limitations of their talents and to develop the patience needed to embrace such an ambivalent situation, allowing them to live in this paradox with a certain peace and joy.

From another perspective, one of the implications of development at the normative level is the necessity of local communities in which significant challenge and support exists. The various means for stimulating conversion, whether from directed retreats, baptisms in the Spirit, spiritual healings, or the like, all need an atmosphere which continually deepens the experience. Berger and Luckmann put it pointedly:

> To have a conversion experience is nothing much. The real thing is to be able to keep on taking it seriously; to retain the sense of its plausibility. *This* is where the religious community comes in. It provides the indispensable plausibility structure for the new reality. (p. 158)

It is in view of this reality that there is a growing conviction that the local community is the primary agent of ongoing formation.

Decline

Poem for Planners

And so I said to him:
"This time, let's decide
Where the tent should
Be, before the circus
Comes down the street."

The poem above would never have been written during the period of development just described. The determination to do something differently "this time" reveals a bittersweet learning from the experience of failure.

Most Americans are taught from childhood that failure is evil, and yet life teaches that unbroken and continual success is impossible. The stabilization period may seem lengthy, but the measure is only relative. History convinces us that change is inevitable and that stabilization marks the end of

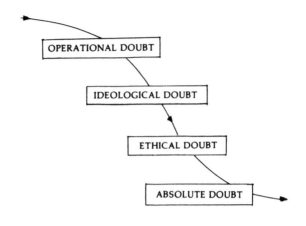

FIGURE 3.3: Decline

development and signals the impending decline (see Figure 3.3). Why is this so?

Sociologists will answer that the inevitable decline is the result of the "utopian flaw" or "the human condition." Theologians will see its cause as "original sin." Bernard Lonergan has aptly described it: "Essentially the problem lies in an incapacity for sustained development."[4] American religious may have difficulty theorizing about the experience, but none will deny that they have felt the anxiety that accompanies descent. This final section of the present chapter will analyze this experience of "death and dying."

"Doubt" is the key analytical word for understanding the various stages of the decline. What kind of doubt is experienced? What is its intensity?

---

[4] Bernard J. F. Lonergan, S.J., *Insight: A Study of Human Understanding*, 3rd ed. (New York: Philosophical Library, 1970), p. 630.

The first expression of doubt begins to be voiced at the thinning edge of the stabilization period. Since to a large extent programs, policies, and norms have lost contact with the founding vision, it is no surprise that the first doubts express concern about these surface realities at the *operational* level. During the stabilization period, basic myths and beliefs are mainly presumed, and perhaps this is why no one thinks to question them at this point. Original deviations from the norms may have resulted from accident, innocence, creativity, or malice, though seldom from the last. Modifying religious garb and moving the place of community prayer from the chapel to the living room are examples of the results of operational doubt. No one yet questions the value of the habit or of community prayer.

A deeper level of breakdown is revealed by doubts concerning the intellectual assumptions that underlie the system. At this level of *ideological* doubt, the fundamental values (myths) that the institution or community embodies are still trusted, though perhaps vaguely understood. The ideology (beliefs), however, or the propositional statements which rationalize and legitimate the social structures and processes undergo critical reexamination. Soon the number of doubters equals the number of those still committed to the system. When religious began to question the need for religious garb and to doubt the necessity of common prayer, they were signalling that the decline had moved to the ideological level. Although there may have been a search through the gospels at this time, or through the life of the founding person, in order to justify these doubts, the relationship to the myth level was still not clearly understood and the "proof texts" were often selective and partial.

A yet deeper level of breakdown has occurred when the expressions of doubt reveal a serious distrust of some of the basic myths and beliefs of the group. At the level of *ethical* doubt, religious begin to question the importance of belonging to one religious family rather than another. That no one can dictate the style of one's prayer becomes an attractive proposition. When ethical doubt is experienced by a group only a radical change affecting the mythology and philosophy of the group will make any difference.

If the downward movement continues, the level of *absolute* doubt marks the complete breakdown in the workability of the system. The institution or system is completely rejected, sometimes sadly, often bitterly. Questions about the value and meaning of religious life or of the possibility of prayer at all signify that the decline in the cycle of religious life has "bottomed out." Although this has not been the case for religious life in general, it has at times been true for individuals and for particular institutes.

It should be pointed out that at any stage in the decline, a reverse in the downward movement can be effected. To experience the levels of ideological and even ethical or absolute doubt may be seen even as a "happy fault." For it is only when the questions are deep enough that the answers can be radical enough to bring about revitalization. Perhaps this is why the "adaptations" made by chapters in the mid-sixties did not succeed in producing real renewal. The turnaround that is made at the deeper levels of doubt will require more time, more searching, more pain. It will probably require assisting at the death of many things cherished; it will be difficult not so much because those things were meaningful but more because they were familiar. The turnaround requires the conversion of life, of individual members, and of the institute—a turning away from death, a turning toward life. It is this experience of personal and communal transformation which makes it possible to touch the deepest level of myth—where revitalization can be rooted.

Chapter Four

The Path of Transformation

IN PREVIOUS CHAPTERS, ISSUES AND MODELS WERE DEVELOPED to enable the exploration of the present status of religious life in the Church. These initial chapters viewed religious life as a charism within the Church, that is, as a gift of God's spirit given for the good of the whole people of God. This inbreaking and movement of the Spirit in history manifests a mysterious pattern of life and growth, death and dying—and rebirth. To give specificity to this pattern of life, death, and resurrection, a historical model for the evaluation of religious life as a movement within the Church was presented in Chapter One.

With this overview as a perspective, the life pattern of an individual community was examined in Chapter Two. Individual communities were seen as charisms in themselves—particular manifestations of the gift of God's Spirit in history. The Vitality Curve of Chapter Three abstracted a number of the underlying themes characteristic of the historical and sociological models. This framework aimed at producing some insight toward the formulation of guidelines for the revitalization of religious life. The Vitality Curve illustrates the interrelationships of a religious vision and the realities of community structures.

The present chapter serves as a bridge between the first and second parts of this book. In it, the theme of the life, death, and rebirth of religious communities is explored through yet another model: the Path of Transformation. This model offers a perspective on religious community as a formal social entity as well as the processes that contribute to major transformations or qualitative changes in the community.

Models such as the Path of Transformation—and others like it—can be helpful in discerning the future to which the Lord is calling religious life. The vitality of religious life as a *social* phenomenon in the Church can never be adequately described in terms of a private or single response to the Lord. The quickening of religious congregations depends on the various structures supporting responsiveness to the Lord. The monumental nature of religious life discloses that the *élan vital* of one religious community is important in animating the existence of other communities. Furthermore, vital and vibrant religious communities have always significantly nurtured the faith of the Church, which reciprocated with its own energizing ministry. Hence the process of discernment and response is a collegial dialogue. If this dialogue is to be fruitful, however, there needs to be agreement on an important set of questions which will be explored within the dialogue. The Path of Transformation is offered as a framework to aid in formulating the questions and sensitizing one to their meanings as a guide in an authentic discernment process of faith and prayer. This total effort creates the context for community transformation.

The second part of this book, then, focuses on guidelines and "tools" that can be used to discover the new facets and trends within the Church and the secular culture that demand a new response. The magnitude and seriousness of the challenges of a major transition in religious life require a relentless pursuit of the processes by which religious communities can shape a response, drawing upon the fertile resources of the tradition of religious life and maintaining its living force by speaking with clarity, decisiveness, and compassion the disquieting message of Christ and his Kingdom.

Community: Strategic Choices and Structures

Religious communities can be viewed from a variety of perspectives. Several chapters in the book have utilized the historical and sociological perspectives. There are also a great number of books today which utilize the theological perspective to discuss the religious life. In this section, a perspective on religious communities as formal social entities, what we might call an organizational perspective, is developed. The development is in terms of the major strategic choices made by the community and the resulting patterns, or what we call structures, that characterize the activities and processes of the community. This perspective is somewhat abstract and makes no claim to completeness, yet it can lead to a clearer appreciation of the dynamics of transformation.

A decision often sets the framework or context for other decisions. For example, if one decides to go to Washington, D.C., then the subsequent decisions to be made, such as the mode of transportation, whether or not to take a heavy coat, etc., are all made within the context of the decision to go to Washington. If one decides to become a medical doctor, then choices of a university, of the type of training, etc., are all made in the context of this career decision. Strategic choices are those choices which a person or group makes that bound all other choices. Hence strategic choices set the fundamental frameworks or contexts for other decisions. People make strategic choices in the choice of career, a marriage partner, etc., and businesses make strategic choices when they decide "what business they are in."

In this organizational perspective, a religious community is seen as being constituted by three interrelated strategic choices, namely, the choice of a gospel venture, the choice of a mode of organizing, and a choice of how to integrate people into the community (see Figure 4.1). Each of these choices is seen to determine or mold the patterns which characterize the activities and processes of the community. The vitality of a religious community can then be characterized by the relative coherence and integration of these choices and the resulting structures. The historical material of Chapters One and Two briefly sketch how religious communities have been constituted by the three strategic choices, namely, a gospel venture, a mode of organizing the community, and the integration of members into the community. The present chapter discusses first the nature of these choices and then the pro-

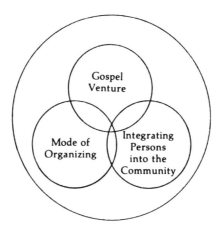

FIGURE 4.1: Interrelated Strategic Decisions

---

cesses by which communities explicitly or implicitly make these choices.

Every charism of a religious community contains a vision or image of the world transformed under the message of the gospel. The term gospel venture is used to indicate the concrete project or enterprise undertaken by the religious community which is inspired by the gospel message and which responds to the historical needs and exigencies of the times. The venture of going out to the desert to do battle with the devil, the venture of building monasteries across Europe, the venture of bringing the world of Christ to the poor and suffering, the venture of defending Christ on any front and expanding his Kingdom to newly discovered lands, and the venture of building institutions (schools and hospitals) for the service of the poor are all manifestations of how vital religious communities throughout history were engaged in a significant gospel venture.

The choice of a gospel venture means that the religious

community has made some choices about the type of service that it wishes to give the Church and the world, the people who will receive this service, the place or geographical location where this service will be given, and the means by which it will be given. The venture is usually a risky enterprise, prone to repeated failure, hardship, and conflict. Yet the venture if successfully completed will have such a desirable impact that much hardship and suffering can be endured in the realization of the venture. The choice of a gospel venture is one of the fundamental frameworks or contexts in which many other community decisions are made. The placement and training of members and the opening and closing of houses all make sense within the framework of the gospel venture.

All of these tasks require coordination if they are to realize the gospel venture. Problematic situations or opportunities must be confronted, information collected about these situations, imaginative alternatives must be considered and evaluated, and eventual choices made. The scarce resources of the community—whether these are people, money, land, or whatever—must be allocated to the different tasks of the community. The interdependence between different decisions and tasks must be attended to so that they all work together toward the accomplishment of the gospel venture. Not only are roles for specialized tasks needed, but there is also a need for roles and processes which bring unity of effort in the realization of the gospel venture. Leadership roles and chapter meetings are some of the ways in which communities work at the tasks of coordination.

A choice of a mode of organizing is a second strategic choice that is made by the religious community. The realization of the gospel venture is a corporate enterprise. It is beyond the efforts of any individual within the community. Hence the work must be divided and members of the community must take on certain roles and specialize in certain activities. Some persons specialize in formation of new members, some specialize in organizing the material necessities of life in common, while others specialize in the work of preaching or teaching. Often, multiple tasks are taken on by an individual person.

The third strategic choice is related to the fact that religious communities are voluntary organizations. This means that members join and remain involved in the community because their personal experiences and commitments are shared by other members of the community and because they can realize their personal goals and aspirations in a significant manner through membership in the community. If the gospel venture of a community and the way that the community organizes to carry out this venture excite people, they will be drawn to join the community. If upon joining the community the gospel venture continues to elicit their commitment and enable the unfolding of their personal aspirations and goals, then they will be motivated to be actively committed to the community.

The method of attracting, inviting, and accepting persons into the community and the methods of forming and training these persons once they are accepted for membership are some of the major processes that a community uses to integrate people into the community. But even after the early years in the community a person's commitment to the community is strengthened by opportunities to develop his/her capacities and competencies, to exercise these in a meaningful way in the realization of the community's gospel venture, and to receive rewards for his/her contributions. It may seem strange to talk about opportunities for self-realization and reward in the context of religious communities which take seriously the gospel counsels. These counsels see self-realization through a self-transcending commitment to the Kingdom of God. Yet it was precisely because some people *sought* such a mode of self-realization and that the gospel venture and mode of organizing of a community *provided* such an opportunity for this mode of self-realization that religious communities were at different times in history so vital.

A reflection on the historical material contained in Chapters One and Two suggests the following assertion about the vitality of religious communities: *Religious communities which have a significant positive impact on the Church and the world and which have committed membership are characterized by a dynamic integration of a gospel venture, of the appropriate modes of organizing, and of the persons who are members of the community.* In vital religious communities the gospel venture must be capable of eliciting the commitment of persons and be realizable through an appropriate structure of human interaction. The community structures must be appropriate for accomplishing the gospel venture and creatively enabling personal contributions to the gospel venture and coordinating these contributions so that it is a community contribution to the gospel venture. Likewise, persons who make up the community must be committed to the gospel venture and capable of organizing the structures of interaction to realize it.

The Dynamics of Transformation

In Chapter Two, the life cycle of individual religious communities was outlined. In that chapter, the cycle was used to illustrate how the life of a religious community evolved through major movements of expansion, stabilization, breakdown, and critical periods. These phases are not distinct and in ways overlap with each other; yet the life cycle provides a helpful approach to understanding and appreciating the history of a particular religious community. It presents a framework for organizing the important events and happenings of the community.

In the life-cycle model, the last two periods (breakdown and critical) made up the transition in the life of religious communities. As was pointed out in Chapter Two, the transition period had three major possible outcomes, namely, extinction, minimal survival, or revitalization. In this section, using a model we call the Path of Transformation, revitalization is studied in a similar manner.

The Path of Transformation, which is shown schematically in Figure 4.2, consists of three major periods (Breakdown and

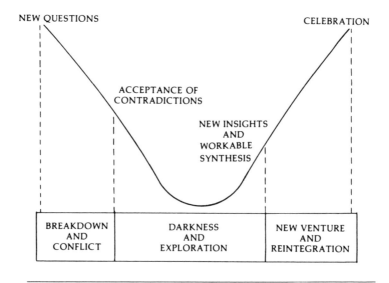

FIGURE 4.2: The Path of Transformation

Conflict, Darkness and Exploration, and New Venture and Reintegration) and four events (New Questions, Acceptance of Contradictions, New Insight and Workable Synthesis, and Celebration) which mark the transitions between periods. Just as the life-cycle model facilitates an understanding and appreciation of this history of the community, the Path of Transformation model should facilitate an understanding and appreciation for each community's journey on the Path of Transformation. The model may give an interpretation to events and situations which are otherwise without meaning and help focus the efforts of communities journeying on the Path of Transformation. The structure of the model was developed from an examination of past historical transformations of religious community and the study of other major social transformations. The examples and anecdotes used to illustrate the model are taken from the present transition of religious life. In this way, the model aids in clarifying the present situation.

1. The Period of Breakdown and Conflict

The major experience in the last ten to fifteen years of religious life has been that of breakdown and disintegration, an experience too little understood in its personal and collective implications. Breakdown and disintegration seem to be the major way the Lord prepares persons and communities for a deep and thorough transformation. This section outlines some of the major dynamics and characteristics of breakdown and disintegration in religious life.

A Boldness in Asking New Questions

The present breakdown period began with a sense of optimism and a sense of growth. In most communities there was a large number of younger people coming into the community and new works were being opened. The future seemed to be assured. Even before the Vatican Council, there seemed to be a new spirit of openness in dealing with the new questions and issues of the modern age. With the documents of the Council there came a series of fresh insights into the nature and life of the Church; the Council opened the Church toward the world in new and startling ways, and opened up issues, such as freedom of conscience, that had been underdeveloped within Church doctrine.

Theology began a new period of growth with an emphasis on doctrinal evolution. The critical phase of the new biblical scholarship, with its emphasis on demythologizing, was being widely heralded. Personalism became a popular philosophical stance for theologizing. The emphasis of these theologies was persons rather than institutions or doctrines. Secular theologies also arose which denied the transcendent-immanent distinction that previously characterized theology. Newer writings on spirituality emphasized incarnational approaches. All of these new trends confronted the traditional formulations of the theology of religious life.

Secular culture was confronting the Church and religious life with a series of new questions. Personalism also became the basis for a new psychology. In the popularization of this psychology the emphasis on human fulfillment and self-actualization was paramount. This new approach raised questions about the practices of religious communities and even whether religious life as such was a psychologically healthy experience. The sexual revolution which began in the sixties was another source of new questions for religious and religious communities.

Modifying Structures

The new questions which challenged religious life led to a serious effort to change structures and customs. The new questions suggested that there were many ways in which the community could be modernized. There were modifications of habits, movements toward a less formally structured life-style, a movement to some small-group living. Old forms of authority and governance were modified to allow for more decentralization and collegiality. Chapters and government structures became more democratic in their proceedings. Moreover, there was new experimentation in the pattern of community prayer.

Disintegrating Spiral of Doubt

In making modifications of the community structures, there was a rising sense of expectation that these modifications would bring a surge of renewal to the community. Yet change was slow and, more often than not, produced failures and confusions. These failures and lack of promise brought a great sense of frustration for those who had hoped for a rapid change. Doubts about the community began to grow. People began to ask whether the beliefs and principles which served as the foundation for the community were any longer valid. Were they not theologically *passé* and no longer sound in a modern Church for a modern world?

During the time of breakdown and conflict, doubt increasingly pervades all dimensions of the community. In the spiral of doubt, major contradictions or dilemmas begin to reveal themselves. There is a tension between personal freedom and fulfillment and the common good of the community, between transcendent and secular commitments, between personal choices of ministry and the needs of the community, and between continuity of traditional works and the responsiveness to new needs.

Basic Issues of the Breakdown

The period of breakdown and conflict in religious communities has several important consequences. First of all, there is a loss of mission and identity. The gospel venture which was once the focus of the community's efforts now seems inappropriate and not responsive to the needs of the times. It is no longer clear what the community stands for and what it is. The important question of why the community exists has no longer the clear and easily understood answer it once had. Polarization weakens the community: person is set in conflict with person, group against group. The bonds of community which during the foundation and expansion periods heightened and realized the contribution of each person and group now turn into patterns of interaction which are conflictual and alienating.

The second important consequence of breakdown is the ambiguity in once-clear community decision and communication processes—such as decisions on the placement of personnel, decisions on what works are to be undertaken, etc. The processes for communicating and making decisions deteriorate and disintegrate, and as a result of this breakdown people feel that they are no longer capable of influencing the community's life in any significant way.

The third consequence of the breakdown in a religious community is the lack of fit between the needs of persons and those of the community's institutional processes. As was seen in previous chapters, members experience religious communities as rigid, inflexible, and unable to meet personal needs. Community institutions, such as chapters and processes of initial and ongoing formation, are now experienced as inhibitors of human and religious growth.

During the periods of the transformation path, it is helpful

TABLE 4.1

- *Stage 1: Denial and Isolation*
  - Flat-out rejection of the distintegration process—not us!
  - Search for ways to fix it.
  - Strong defenses.

- *Stage 2: Anger*
  - Anger, rage, envy, and resentment: Why should I/we be suffering a deep disintegration?
  - Anger is displaced in all directions and projected into the environment.
  - The best laid plans must go by the wayside. I/we must let go of something.
  - Loss of a sense of control—a feeling of extreme helplessness.

- *Stage 3: Bargaining*
  - Is there a slim chance that if I/we change some behaviors, there will be a grant of reprieve from a deep disintegration of the self or the community?
  - Bargaining is an attempt to postpone the inevitable.
  - If only I/we pray or work harder God will send novices.

- *Stage 4: Depression*
  - Depression coming from a sense of loss.
  - Something must be left behind.
  - The need to separate oneself or the community from former securities.

- *Stage 5: Acceptance*
  - A willingness to accept a passover journey.

for persons and communities to have symbols and metaphors which can meaningfully interpret the experience of the period. Elisabeth Kübler-Ross and others have explored the dynamics of the personal confrontation with death and dying. Table 4.1 lists the five-stage description of the processes and suggests ways that they might be experienced by persons and communities during disintegration.

2. The Period of Darkness and Exploration

A Major Milestone: Acceptance of Contradictions

The second major period in the Path of Transformation is that of darkness and exploration. The community realizes a major milestone when it can recognize and accept the major contradictions that have become manifest during the time of breakdown and conflict. The community must be willing to admit that its present life and structures are not personally satisfying for a significant number of people and that they no longer represent an appropriate response to the major needs of the Church and the world. Although this acceptance does not bring a resolution to the contradictions and dilemmas it does represent a commitment to search for a resolution to these issues. The acceptance of contradictions is a letting go of an "old way" and a starting of a journey to a "new way."

A Time of Personal Exploration

The period of darkness and exploration is also a time when an individual begins a search for personal transformation. This search is a search for a new relationship with Christ, a new depth in prayer and faith, and a new openness to the call of the Lord. The acceptance of contradictions of the community and living within the tensions of these contradictions prepares the way for transformation. Yet this sought-after transformation will come only after a long period of *personal* darkness and exploration. The frustration or dissatisfaction with the community during the time of breakdown challenges a person to exploration of personally unknown and uncharted ways of faith and prayer. For a number of people, the period of search and exploration is marked with a shattering experience of doubt, uncertainty, and pain.

The religious who courageously undertakes the exploration is truly in the experience of a dark night. Old identities which gave meaning in previous years are diffused and undone. The community structures which once defined relatedness and essential stabilites have broken apart. Yet deep faith, courage, and commitment by the religious allow himself or herself to be open to the Spirit. From the purification of this time of darkness and the openness to the Spirit comes the realization that a conscious, deliberate, and organized effort is needed to create a more satisfying community. Hope—the desire for what is not yet—begins to grow within members of the community.

This period is marked by a regrounding of persons and the community in the biblical roots of religious life. The scriptures are prayerfully explored for an experience of the Lord and his Kingdom which will be the basis for a deeper commitment and insight for the rebuilding of community life.

The study of community documents, both foundational and contemporary, which was once distasteful, is undertaken by a number of persons. In prayerful reflections over these documents, people attempt to understand the religious experience that was at the foundation of the community.

The Struggles of Exploration

By accepting the contradictions of the present within their life, communities are able to search for a new life. This time of darkness is a time of exploring without insight. It is a time of patience and waiting, a time characterized by experimentation. But it is an experimentation that is more of a probing of the darkness than an enlightened plan of action. Changes are made in a search for patterns of community life that are a more life-giving and satisfying interaction.

Discovery of a new gospel venture requires that a community have processes for searching and experimenting. These processes will allow the community to be exposed to new variations in its life and its work, thereby increasing the likelihood that new patterns will be found that are more attractive and more satisfying to the members, responsive to the needs of the world and the Church, and better suited to the charism of the community. This process of experimentation and searching will allow groups within the community to experiment with new roles and functions of ministry within the Church and new styles and modes of local community living. Individual people within the community will take on ministries which differ from the traditional ministry of the community. People will experience new styles of living together and of becoming a community of prayer. Also, the processes of searching and experimenting should challenge individual persons to modify the basic patterns of their own life, to experiment with new modes of behaving which will allow them to develop more satisfying patterns of activity.

The search and experimentation process has built into it a basic tension. On one hand, the more numerous the experiments and variations of the community's pattern are during the period of transition, the more likely the community will be able to discover new innovative patterns which will make it satisfying to its members and, in the long run, a vital community. On the other hand, if the rate of experimentation and searching progresses too rapidly it will undermine the basic stability and sustainability of the community. The process of searching and experimenting must somehow balance both of these dimensions.

The process of experimenting and searching—whether in the development of scientific knowledge, in the process of human learning, or in the process of social change—always involves more errors and failures, at least initially, than it involves successes. One of the important skills that will be necessary in this time of searching is the ability to be comfortable with error and with one's mistakes, and the ability to learn from these mistakes. To be successful in the search and experimentation process, a community must be error-embracing as opposed to error-denying. If the process is entered upon with the expectation of never making a mistake, the person or community will not be able to maintain a very creative process of search and experimentation.

The process emphasizes diversity and pluralism within the

group. Such diversity and pluralism seem to enhance the likelihood that fundamental innovations will emerge within the community. Hence, members must be able to live with a certain degree of ambiguity. They must be willing to accept diversity and pluralism as a condition for the eventual vitality of a religious community.

Many have suggested that the searching and experimentation process in religious life should be planned, purposeful, and goal-oriented. The major difficulty with this suggestion is that experiments and variations in life styles can only be planned, purposeful, and goal-oriented in view of an already achieved wisdom of the community. Fundamental innovations somehow both break out of and enhance this traditional wisdom. If all experimentation is restricted to traditional wisdom, the chances of finding a significant innovation that will insure the vitality of the community are minimized. It is from the unexpected or the effective surprise that reality is seen in a new way.

3. The Period of New Venture and Reintegration

A Major Milestone: New Insight and Workable Synthesis

One of the major prerequisites for the movement of a religious community from a time of search and darkness to that of creating a transformed community is the personal transformation among a significant number of people in the community. Transformation here means that the collapsed inner world of meaning is resynthesized through a religious experience which brings about a fundamental, personal conversion and reorientation of life. The most striking feature of this metanoia is a new (in the sense of deeper, broader, etc.) relationship to the person of Jesus and the gospel message of the Kingdom.

The conversion experience reorients the total life of the person, manifesting itself in some of the following ways:

• perception is changed, new realities are noticed that were not noticed before, and some things which were once interpreted as important are no longer seen that way;

• there are new insights into the contemporary world, its problems and needs;

• the conversion calls forth a commitment to a new way of acting.

Through the mutual interaction of the new interpretation of life and the consequent new ways of acting, a relatively stable yet altered set of attitudes emerges, perhaps regarding modes of presence to the poor and unwanted, or ways of spiritual growth and methods of prayer. This process of transformation is usually a slow process, although the acknowledgement of this transformation may be concentrated in a few major judgments and decisions.

A Revitalization Network

If true revitalization is to occur, transformation must go beyond the personal. It must penetrate and reshape the entire social reality of the institute. A critical step in the revitalization process is the coalescence of those members who have experienced a deep change into a network through which that conversion experience is sustained and enhanced. In the sharing of their "stories," awareness will deepen and intensify and become a mutual vision and commitment. This group—and the links between its members may be both formal and informal—gradually becomes an animating force dedicated to building more rewarding community experiences and recovering the gripping attraction to living according to Christ's conditions of evangelical discipleship.

An important moment in this transformation is the emergence of images, symbols, and metaphors which integrate and give meaning to the regenerated inner world. Critical reflection on the images and metaphors will help to clarify their meaning and evaluate their importance in the process of remythologizing and reappropriating the founding charism. And if indeed this is the work of the Spirit, an atmosphere of healing and reconciliation will prevail.

Through the revitalization network, persons recognize that they are capable of creating their own history. The "congregational conversation" alluded to in Chapter Three begins on a small scale and echoes throughout the community. But it is not just talk. The conviction grows and leads to action—steps to building new community structures that are "plausibility structures," as Berger and Luckmann state: "The most important social condition [for transformation] is the availability of an effective plausibility structure, that is, a social base serving as the 'laboratory' of transformation."[1]

Fundamental Innovations

The personal transformation and the emergence of a revitalization network are not simply for the development of a cozy coterie of the saved. Rather these steps are in turn themselves prerequisites to the generation of fundamental innovations in the community structures of life and ministry. These innovations must be multiple and touch basic dimensions of the community, such as initial and ongoing formation, local community life, spirituality, government, and ministry.

While there is always the danger of an arrogance and an elitism (and there will undoubtedly be such charges no matter what the reality), the authenticity of the conversion will be manifested in the simple freedom of members maintaining—and being enriched by—ongoing membership in various groups in the congregation. Another expression will be the multiple roles of leadership in the revitalization network.

Diffusion of Innovations

If the fundamental innovations that arise are to become established in the community, it is necessary that the new ventures be given approval by the leadership of the congregation. Not the least manifestation of this approval will be in the form of recognition, and in human and financial resources. As these innovations respond to personal and apostolic needs, the general interest in innovative restructuring rises and not only expands the revitalization network but

---

[1] Peter L. Berger and Thomas Luckmann, *The Social Construction of Reality* (Garden City, N.Y.: Doubleday, Anchor Books, 1976), p. 157.

also extends the innovative leadership throughout the community.

As the innovations grow, take shape, and stabilize, they form a set of coherent patterns within the community which people can understand and commit themselves to. The cluster of innovations that emerge will represent a "new venture" for the institute. At this time it becomes important for community structures to facilitate learning and discernment. Significant among these will be the presence of a leadership with high tolerance for ambiguity and conflict, low need for approval—and dogged persistence.

The commitment occasioned by the "new venture" benefits the revitalization by bringing about a sense of shared identity and purpose. As the common basis of understanding grows, dialogue is enhanced—hence a new sense of integration. Such a basis of commitment can thus undergird changes in the crucial structures of decision making, such as personnel placement and the allotment of resources. However, if these fundamental innovations are to be long-lasting and integral, the processes of initial and ongoing formation must be so revamped as to reinforce the new modes of living and serving.

In this time in its history, religious life is aided in the understanding of its Path of Transformation by the emergence in the social sciences of the deepened and refined understanding of adult-life development. A graphic summary of the primary thrust of this chapter is provided by Figure 4.3. The description focuses on the major periods and transitional events of the individual adult life, but the relation to the "corporate person" of the religious congregation is obvious.

Creating the Context for Community Transformation

Chapters Five and Six outline some tools that can be used by groups within the local community or the community at large to work at the process of transformation. The Vitality Curve outlined in Chapter Three is helpful in organizing some questions that the community must be concerned with in the

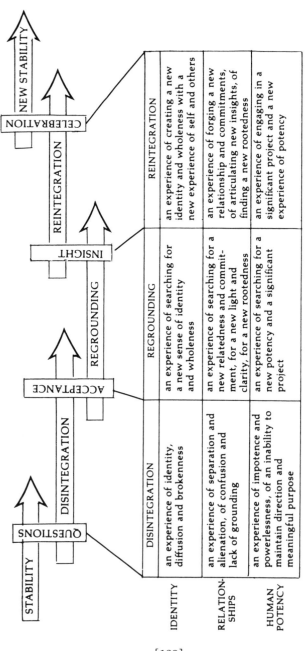

	DISINTEGRATION	REGROUNDING	REINTEGRATION
IDENTITY	an experience of identity, diffusion and brokenness	an experience of searching for a new sense of identity and wholeness	an experience of creating a new identity and wholeness with a new experience of self and others
RELATION-SHIPS	an experience of separation and alienation, of confusion and lack of grounding	an experience of searching for a new relatedness and commitment, for a new light and clarity, for a new rootedness	an experience of forging a new relationship and commitments, of articulating new insights, of finding a new rootedness
HUMAN POTENCY	an experience of impotence and powerlessness, of an inability to maintain direction and meaningful purpose	an experience of searching for a new potency and a significant project	an experience of engaging in a significant project and a new experience of potency

STABILITY — QUESTIONS — DISINTEGRATION — ACCEPTANCE — REGROUNDING — INSIGHT — REINTEGRATION — CELEBRATION — NEW STABILITY

FIGURE 4.3: Transformation and Adult Life

process of transformation. Figure 4.4 attempts to display some of these concerns.

The far left column outlines major dimensions of community meaning developed in Chapter Three: myths, beliefs, and norms.

myths: the imaginative stories that capture the inner meaning of human life and which constitute the paradigm for all significant actions for the community; they recount and celebrate how important dimensions of the community came into existence.

beliefs: the shared set of understandings that members have about themselves, their relationship with other groups, and similar matters.

norms: the stable pattern of expectations and actions in both the life and ministerial aspects of the community.

The middle column illustrates the roles that must be assumed by different members in the community if the process of transformation is to be successful. The roles needed include those people who are able to create new visions for the community, those who are able to articulate this vision in a language and in conceptual frameworks that are meaningful to contemporary persons, and those who are able to create and organize these structures of the community life and the community ministry based on the articulation. Yet, no one person could fulfill or be skillful in all the roles that are needed for the transformation of the community. Most likely, some people within the community will have a more prominent and more visible leadership role; nevertheless the work of transformation must be a widespread phenomenon. One of the most significant challenges in organizing the transformational process is that of actualizing all the roles that are needed within the community.

The prophets and sensitizers are those people within the community who are able to anticipate the new situation to which the community must respond, as well as the new responses the community must make in these new situations. Community story tellers and myth makers are those who are

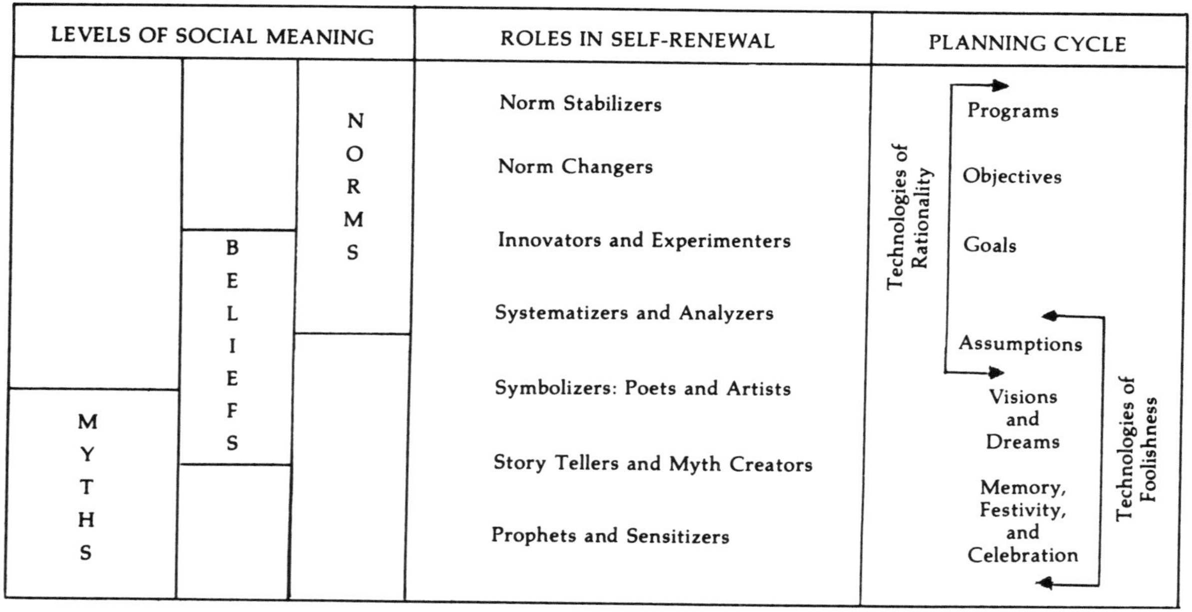

LEVELS OF SOCIAL MEANING	ROLES IN SELF-RENEWAL	PLANNING CYCLE
N O R M S	Norm Stabilizers	Programs
	Norm Changers	Objectives
B E L I E F S	Innovators and Experimenters	Goals
	Systematizers and Analyzers	Assumptions
	Symbolizers: Poets and Artists	Visions and Dreams
M Y T H S	Story Tellers and Myth Creators	Memory, Festivity, and Celebration
	Prophets and Sensitizers	

Technologies of Rationality

Technologies of Foolishness

FIGURE 4.4: Self-Renewal in Communities

able to recount for the community the experience of the wondrous ways that the Lord has broken in and touched the community in the past and transformed the life of the community as it searched for new responses. The community poets and artists create community symbols through their ability to develop images and metaphors which allow the experience of the Lord's presence within the community to be communicated and shared among the members.

The systematizers and analyzers are those persons within the community who are able to bring critical and reflective thought to the myths and symbols of the community and, through critical reflection, to discover new and meaningful articulations of what the community is about. The innovators and experimenters are capable of formulating new ways of structuring community life and new projects for the community ministry.

The norm changers create the new patterns of interaction within the community which allow new projects and new experiments to be successfully implemented. The norm stabilizers are those who are capable of stabilizing new patterns of interaction and structures within the community so that the new projects and experiments are able to remain as an ongoing part of the community life.

The third column outlines the dimensions of the community planning cycle. As we mentioned in the Introduction, the process of transformation will require the integration and synthesis of both the rational and nonrational bases of human thought and action. The bottom half of the planning cycle touches mostly on the nonrational dimensions of community transformation: memory, festivity, and celebration, as well as visions and dreams. All of these aspects are articulated in a set of assumptions, and it is important for the planning work of the community to include opportunities for celebration and for rituals through which the community can remember important moments of community and personal life. The approaches to the technology of foolishness that are outlined in Chapter Five begin to offer some guidelines for the nonrational dimensions of planning. To be a transformed community, the members must be willing to learn to be playful and foolish.

The nonrational basis of community development needs to be integrated with rational methods of organizing and reflection. Memories, dreams, and visions provide a powerful basis for the transformation of community structures and the development of fundamental innovations, but they must work hand in hand with the art of rationality. In Chapter Six, a process of program planning is outlined which can serve as a guideline for communities in the implementation of the process of transformation. The planning process is organized around four major ideas: dialogue, decision, action, and evaluation. These four words give some insight in understanding the patterns of action of the community.

Dialogue examines the ways the community develops a common way of understanding and valuing its life and mission, as well as the issues and problems that it must address through its actions. The question of the decision phase asks how a community comes to design those desired futures and creates pathways to reach them. Action focuses on the actual means the community uses to go about moving toward the desired future along the pathways that are chosen. Finally, evaluation focuses on a mode for communal learning through action and reflection on action, so as to better understand the meaning of the steps taken.

The planning cycle of the community should attempt to integrate both empirical facts (hard facts) with intuitive and imaginative facts (soft facts). The planning cycle of a community attempts to integrate past, present, and future. It must develop pathways which incorporate the trends and living conditions of the past, the experience and constraints of the present, and the visions for the future. The community planning cycle must also be participative: developing the multitude of channels needed to involve a variety of persons within the community in the process of providing information, making decisions, implementing plans and projects, as well as learning new things from these actions.

The planning cycle of a community ought to be coordinated, in that all aspects of the community should be planning simultaneously and interdependently. All aspects of the community need to be interrelated in the search and development of a common thrust. The planning cycle within a community must be continuous. Goals and objectives, visions and dreams need to be continuously examined in the light of present experience.

Figure 4.4 can serve as a summary and reminder of important questions to guide the organizing of the transformational process. Are all the levels of community meaning touched? Have real attempts been made to actualize the wide spectrum of talents from within the community that are needed for transformation, or has the renewal process deadened or alienated certain types of people? Is the community organizing both the rational and the nonrational dimensions of the communal transformation process?

Chapter Five

The Technologies of Foolishness

THE EXISTENTIAL BASIS FOR THIS CHAPTER DERIVES FROM THE experience of the authors in working with religious groupings. In conducting various kinds of workshops and numerous consultancies, the use of technologies of foolishness has proven to be one of the keys to success. This has occurred not only with individual religious communities, but in the Leadership Conference of Women Religious, sisters' senate representatives on a statewide level, diocesan commissions on religious, and similar organizations. The theory presented and the strategies suggested have been "tested" and found to be effective in the process of revitalization.

Another perspective of this chapter is the present reading of the signs of the times, which signal the end of the Modern Era (which lasted from about 1600 to 1950). The Modern Era was dominated by an exaggerated version of the rationalist bias that has infected Western civilization from the time of the Greeks. In the Modern Era, this bias took the peculiar form of an infatuation with great rational systems or structures. Expressions of this emphasis can be found in Cartesian philosophy, Newtonian physics, nationalism in government, capitalism and communism in economics, as well as in the ballet and the symphony in the arts.

One of the signs that the Modern Era is coming to an end is that today people can palpably feel the inadequacy of the rational techniques for dealing with the contemporary malaise in all dimensions of society. This inadequacy is evident in our inability to be nonrational, which follows from being children of the Modern Era whether we like it or not.

The technologies of foolishness are relevant to this situation. The structure of the human mind which gives rise to memory and hope finds expression in the "serious playfulness" of the technologies of foolishness, just as it does in that mysterious process called dreaming.

It should be clear that the process of community learning and discerning involves more than rationality. Whenever there is talk of "dialogue," "discernment," or "barriers," the nonrational is woven into the fabric such that the texture is that of lived life. This is perhaps even more evident in the various designs that use the contingency approach to learning and discerning.

The notion of "contingency," that is, the belief that rationality and nonrationality must be balanced in approaches to revitalization, grows out of the assumption that it is of the essence of a religious congregation, as it is of the entire Church, to be *community*, not simply *institution*. The consequences of this distinction are bound up with a relaxed understanding that the "utopian flaw" or the "effects of original sin" season life together, adding not only the spice of variety, but also the eruptions of laughter, tears, care, and anger—all of which must be blended with that touch of foolishness that St. Paul speaks of in his first letter to the Corinthians.

The Bias of Foolishness

As one begins to read the literature on modern organizational and management theory, one is surprised to find that there is very little mention of religious communities as organizations in that literature. It is surprising because religious communities have been around for a long time and have endured longer than most other organizations. There is often some mention of authoritarian structures, which are supposed to be typical of most religious communities; and the formation processes which initiate people into religious communities are typically defined as coercive socialization processes. Yet these stereotypical remarks do not capture the fullness of what religious communities have been as organizations. Perhaps this is because the theories of modern management planning and organizational theory do not quite mesh as easily with religious communities as with other organizations, such as business and government.

These two problems—the absence of a description of religious communities in management and organizational theory, and the lack of fit between modern theories of planning, organizing, and managing with the realities of religious communities—point out a deep bias in organizational literature, namely, the bias of rationality.

The bias of rationality is fundamental and pervades every aspect of our culture, its organizations, and its social systems. The major tenets of this bias run something like this: Human beings in groups are always confronted with situations involving choice. If done properly, these choices are made by evaluating alternatives in terms of the goals of the group and on the basis of information currently available. That alternative which is most attractive in terms of the group goals is the one that is chosen. The process of making choices may be improved by utilizing the technologies of rationality, such as planning and modern management techniques. Through these technologies, groups can improve the quality of their search for an alternative, the quality of information available to them, and the quality of analysis that they use to evaluate alternatives. Although actual choices may fall short of this ideal in many ways, it is an attractive model for how groups should make choices. (Chapter Six will explore the processes of rationality and the action planning that flows from it.)

In the last decade, the theory of complex systems and the theory of environmental uncertainty have supplemented and enhanced the basic bias of rationality which pervades modern planning, organizing, and managing. Yet, even in the midst of extreme complexity and uncertainty, it is usually assumed that a person has complete knowledge of the alternatives and possesses some measure or yardstick of the utility which allows the assignment of preference of one alternative over another. Accordingly, there is also assumed the ability to choose one of the alternatives which maximize this notion of utility.

However, religious communities have by their nature a bias of foolishness. They are most often founded in the context of myth and mystery by persons who appear odd, in that they purport to "know" something of the eternal salvific plan, in order to make a contribution to this common quest. With an aplomb that risks and receives ridicule, these founding persons and their communities embody a spirit which does not so much give rise to radically new capacities as it leavens with the power of the Spirit charisms that belong to the fullness of humankind. The foolishness of the new endeavor is in the simplicity of a new power and end.

As the foundation period turns to expansion and stabilization, the religious congregations apply the processes of rationality in developing the internal community policy, in organizing the ministries to enable the charism, and in reflecting on how well the common purposes have been carried out. Yet the methods that spring from the bias of rationality cannot be the sole means for planning, implementing, or evaluating in religious life. Its origin and sources of "power," as well as its ultimate imperative goal of building a kingdom that is somehow not entirely of this world, give it a bias for the foolishness of becoming "a spectacle to the universe, to angels and men alike. We are fools on Christ's account" (1 Cor. 4:9–10).

And since the vowed life is part of the radical lifestyle that enables the mission of the congregation, religious life is foolish from its matrix—because it is "unnatural." How does one explain celibacy *for the Kingdom*, or for that matter any renunciation, in a rational way without arriving at an unexplainable social surd? That there are plausible "this-worldly" reasons is clear, but *for the Kingdom!* The "not of this world" aspect of faith (which is foundational to religious life) precludes "worldly" or rational explanations for the call and response known as religious life from being totally adequate.

However, it should be said that foolishness and rationality can be complementary. The technologies of foolishness are usually used by the authors preliminary to beginning the planning cycle in a workshop setting. The effect of these processes is to create community unity and reveal meanings and myths that may be beneath the conscious level. In the midst of this, opportunities emerge for building trust and developing supportive relationships. If these latter dimensions of group life are not attended to, then the positive aspects of rationality will not see the light of day.

The bias of rationality assumes the preexistence and purpose of the organization, the necessity of its members acting in a consistent manner, and the primacy of rationality in all of its actions. The bias of foolishness recognizes the ever-becoming of the community, asks how in exploring inconsistent behavior new goals might be discovered, and relaxes in a faith posture with the primacy of the nonrational dimensions of human life.

Some Technologies of Foolishness

The following are some examples of technologies of foolishness that the authors have successfully used in various situations. Some are more structured than others; some are more original, others are freely adapted. The final one, "Dialogue with the Founding Person," for example, is a simple variation on an exercise in *At a Journal Workshop* by Ira Progoff (New York: Dialogue House Library, 1975, pp. 158ff.). More about devising technologies of foolishness follows the exercises.

Historicizing

Purpose: The purpose of this exercise is fivefold:
    a) to develop awareness that our "story" is carried in individual members, and that members of different age groups have shared different chapters of that story;
    b) to help each member own *our* story as *his/her* story;

c) to demonstrate that our story is not only found in the formal history and records of the congregation;

d) to raise consciousness in each member that one's own personal history has affected and been affected by the community's history;

e) to prompt us to ask questions of meaning from our shared history.

Process: Small groups, each having a (participant) recorder. Sharing in large group through reporters.

Materials: Newsprint (two or three sheets for each group) or large sheets of paper (approximately 24″ × 40″); felt-tip markers; masking tape.

Time: Twenty-five to forty minutes for small groups; fifteen to twenty-five minutes for sharing in the large group. Time depends on the size and number of small groups. Time should be long enough to allow story telling but short enough to preserve interest and excitement.

DESCRIPTION

1. Participants are divided into small groups. Each small group is provided with two or three large sheets of paper and two felt-tip markers. Each group selects a recorder to write the events mentioned by participants.

2. A line is drawn across the middle of the paper, lengthwise. The date of the current year is written at the left side of the line.

3. Participants are asked to recall significant events in the life of the congregation beginning with the present and going back as far as anyone in the group is able to recall. A significant event is an event after which life was changed for the congregation. Not all such significant events find their way into formal histories. Sometimes, in fact, they have been suppressed! Participants should be urged to recall events which they perceive as significant, and these events are listed above the line, giving at least general dates.

4. After the groups have listed community events, each participant should be urged to recall and list events that are

significant in their personal lives as well. These are recorded below the line, beginning with the current year, and giving dates.

5. After all events have been recorded, the groups are asked to reflect on what they have recorded and to respond to the question, "What is the meaning to be drawn from this history?" These meaning statements should be recorded on a separate large sheet.

6. In the large group, volunteers from each small group share the results of this exercise. Sharing of meaning statements is particularly helpful.

The Dream Trip

Purpose: The purpose of this exercise is twofold:
  a) to enable the group to build images of its future;
  b) to enable the group to critically examine the hopes and fears that are embodied in the collective images.

Process: Small groups, each having a (participant) recorder. Sharing in large group through reporters.

Materials: Newsprint (two or three sheets for each group) or large sheets of paper (approximately 24" × 40"); felt-tip markers; masking tape.

Time: Approximately thirty minutes for the small groups and fifteen minutes for the sharing. Time depends on the size and number of small groups.

DESCRIPTION

1. Participants are divided into small groups. Each small group is provided with two to four sheets of newsprint (which are to be taped together to provide sufficient area) and a felt-tip marker. Each group selects a recorder.

2. A branched time line (see diagram) is drawn on the newsprint.

3. A specific date in the future is chosen to represent the end of the time lines. Five or ten years from the present date is usually a good time to pick.

4. Starting with the bottom line, the group lists all of the events that would occur if the worst possible future for the

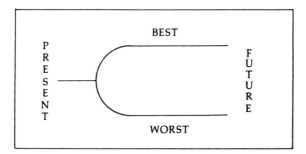

group were to occur. Specific descriptions and dates should be used.

5. Moving to the top line, the group lists all of the events that would occur if the best possible future for the group were to occur. Again specific descriptions and dates should be used.

6. Taking another sheet of newsprint the group makes two lists. The first list contains the completion of the sentence "Our greatest fears and doubts are . . ." and the second list contains the completion of the sentence "Our hopes and dreams are . . . ."

7. In the large group, volunteers from each small group share the results of this exercise. General discussion may follow on similarities, dissimilarities, patterns, or trends.

Variations:

1. The future focused upon by the group may be limited to the particular function or area of responsibility of the participants.

2. This exercise often works well following upon the "Historicizing" exercise previously described. If so, one of the meaning statements generated might serve as the focus of the future.

3. Participants may be asked to write down some of their bests and worsts before sharing and recording them in the small group. This manner is particularly helpful if the facilitator determines that dominant personality types un-

duly influence the group, suppressing contributions from others.
4. The exercise may be successfully used without step 6 of the process.

Twenty Questions

Purpose: The purpose of this exercise is to enable the participants to surface and reflect on their perceptions of the identity of the community or group. The exercise also helps to develop shared appreciation and valuing.

Process: Individually, then in dyads or small groups. If appropriate, small-group consensus can be shared in large group.

Materials: One prepared sheet for each participant; pencils.

Time: Fifteen minutes for individual work; fifteen or twenty minutes in dyads or small groups. Additional time for sharing in large group, if desired.

DESCRIPTION

1. A sheet is prepared containing the following statement twenty times:

    The Sisters of (N.) are _____
    _____.

2. Each participant is asked to complete the twenty statements privately.
3. In dyads or small groups, the participants share their completed statements.
4. If useful, the small groups can make consensus lists and share them through a reporter in the large group.

Variations:

1. This exercise can be done first by individuals completing the statement "I am _____" or "I have a gift for _____." This enables each one to reflect on his/her own charisms or gifts. This step could then be followed by the exercise above. The sharing of the individual completions helps to awaken an appreciation of the multifaceted nature of the community's charism. Followed by the exer-

cise described above, the interrelation of one's personal life with the life of the community is highlighted.

2. This exercise can also be employed profitably to develop mutual appreciation among several congregations in a diocese or region. Members of each congregation complete the exercise "The Sisters of (N.) are _____" and share the responses. Each participant or each small group can then complete twenty statements, "The Sisters of (diocese or region) are _____." These results can then be shared in the large group to develop a heightened awareness of the gifts of communities engaged in common projects or apostolates.

Dialogue with the Founding Person

Purpose: Following the line of thought suggested by Progoff, the purpose of this exercise is to enable the participants to explore in a dialogical manner their relationship with a person with whom they feel "connection of inner importance" in their lives, and with whom the relationship may have "some further step of development or clarification" that might be taken. The founding person is suggested as the other party for the dialogue; however, if this is not appropriate, another person may be chosen.

Process: Individually, then shared at the person's discretion in a small and/or large group.

Materials: Paper and pencil for each participant.

Time: At least thirty to forty-five minutes for writing the dialogue script.

DESCRIPTION

1. Once the person to be dialogued with is chosen, the participant should spend some quiet time getting in touch with that person through reflection on the person's life, words, or their existing relationship. This is often best done in some relatively private place or space.

2. After some time, the dialogue script is begun. Either party may begin with whatever comes, as it comes, speaking and listening, recording in an unconditional manner. It is

usually helpful to write the founding person's name or "me" at the margin of the paper as the dialogue begins and continues.

3. As much as is possible, the participants should be urged to let the script "write itself," i.e., letting it go where it will without conscious guidance, whether it appears rational or not or even whether or not the participant consciously agrees with it.

4. After sufficient time is allowed for the writing (do not rush this, as it is often a very moving experience) the group may be gathered and opportunity may be given for sharing the script. It is important that no one is pressured into reading, nor should there be comment or discussion on what is read. At some later time, the group might reflect together on the experience of writing the dialogue script.

Reflection on Charism

This exercise should be done privately and prayerfully by individual members. How each one experienced this exercise and the responses arrived at might then be profitably shared in a small group.

In a quiet place, spend a short time in silence, recall the presence of God, and reflect prayerfully on your life and vocation.

In this spirit, meditate slowly on each of the following questions:

1. What gifts was I aware of having when I entered religious life?
2. Has there been an increased awareness in me of my gifts since I entered this community? Am I aware of new gifts?
3. Did I then, or do I now, sense an identity between my gifts and what I perceive as the community's charism?
4. Which of my gifts are apostolic in character? Which could be?
5. Do I experience my gifts as "call"?
6. Which of my sisters' gifts am I aware of? Am I aware of my sisters individually as gifted?

7. Which of may sisters' gifts are apostolic? Which could be?
8. What difficulty have I experienced in responding to these questions? What caused this difficulty?
9. What do I need to do to be able to respond to these questions?
10. What do we need to do as a community to respond to these questions?

Inventing Technologies of Foolishness

So far in this chapter the bases for technologies of foolishness have been examined and some examples of them laid out. But perhaps in the long run this section will be the most important, as the complexity and variety of situations often demand invention. The contention here is that it is easy enough to invent or adapt technologies of foolishness if one has a framework from which ask: "What am I trying to do?"

In a word the answer to the question is: Generate an integrating nonrational experience. Basically a technology of foolishness is a way of allowing people to surface their inner and outer experiences, share them with others, and then try to understand their meaning as a way of moving toward decisions which are new goals. Louis M. Savory, S.J., in *Integrating Values* (Dayton: Pflaum Publishing, 1974) outlines a simple framework which can be used for the above purposes. Briefly, Savory (making use of Bernard Lonergan's work) speaks of four levels of consciousness evident in the process of decision making: *experience,* or the person's inner or outer stimuli; *understanding,* or the attribution of meaning to the experience; *judgment,* which assigns value and preference to what is experienced and understood; and *decision,* which translates the above into action.

Not all situations will require an exercise that uses all of the aspects of the above framework. But the "inventor" or facilitator asks several questions. Given the situation at hand, what is the focus of reflection for the group? Is it the community charism, its history, an area of its apostolate, etc.? What sort of experience can be fashioned which will touch or resonate with the nonrational dimensions of the participants? How can these feelings, beliefs, attitudes, or values be generated and then shared (usually) with others? What new decisions do the results point to?

The resources for inventing or adapting technologies of foolishness are manifold. One might share the model with the participants and draw upon their own competencies to structure the event. Groups which include educators, community organizers, administrators and the like contain a wealth of potential. This method has the advantages of building commitment to the process and broadening the scope of available means.

The recent literature from the field of human-relations training and the behavioral sciences affords a plentiful supply of ideas. Below is a selected list of resources that the authors have found particularly helpful.

VALUES CLARIFICATION

A Handbook of Practical Strategies, by Simon, Howe & Kirschenbaum. New York: Hart Publishing, 1972.

SIMULATION GAMING

Simulation Sharing Service, Box 1176, Richmond, Virginia 23209.

Simile II, P.O. Box 1023, La Jolla, California 92037. Free catalogue available; distributes *The Guide to Simulation Games,* by Zuckerman and Horn.

Brite Games, Box 371, Moline, Illinois 61265. Free catalogue.

GROUP FACILITATION AND STRUCTURED EXPERIENCES

University Associates, 7596 Eads Avenue, La Jolla, California 92037. Distributes "Annual Handbook for Group Facilitators," "Handbook of Structured Experiences for Human Relations Training," and *Instrumentation in Human Relations Training,* by Pfieffer and Heslin.

PERSONALITY SURVEYS

"The Gray-Wheelwright Test," a Jungian-type survey. Society of Jungian Analysts, San Francisco, California.

"Meyers-Briggs Type Indicator," from Educational Testing Service, Princeton, New Jersey 08540.

Memory and hope as a theme in the revitalization of religious life calls for creative interaction. Technologies of foolishness, because they can bring persons and communities to their fundamental myths and meanings, provide effective processes in the journey to the future.

Chapter Six

Action Planning and the Art of Rationality

THE ABILITY OF A RELIGIOUS COMMUNITY TO RENEW AT THE level of belief and myth was explored through the bias of foolishness. The purpose of this chapter is to introduce methods of rational decision making and planning which can help a community to renew at the level of expectations and actions, i.e., the level of norms. The bias of rationality will add another tool which can be used in the revitalization of religious life. Methods described in this chapter have been developed through working with many religious communities at the task of renewal. The planning methods are issue-oriented in nature, designed for use in small groups, and useful in fostering decisions with a short time frame. Initially, the chapter briefly explores some general aspects of rationality and planning. Then the Dialogue/Decision/ Action/Evaluation (DDAE) model of planning is used to formulate a practical application of the bias of rationality.

In order to make the ideas more concrete, the experience of a particular order is outlined in a step-by-step illustration. The case history involves a midwestern province of a religious order of women. The authors are particularly familiar with the efforts of a group designed to research and plan in the area of government. Throughout the chapter, the examples used are from this experience.

The meetings of commissions, committees, boards, and teams have become a common occurrence in religious communities today. These task-oriented groups, which come together for the purpose of confronting a problem, issue, or opportunity, provide the occasions for planning. In this setting, people are called upon to respond to some condition in their environment and to organize, create, and shape alternative responses to that condition. Action planning is a systematic and rational way to deal with ordinary problems. For example, a group might be assembled to find a solution to the financial problems of a retreat center; a provincial team might come together to decide on the best strategy for community visitations; or the formation team might meet to deal with the demands of ongoing formation. The application of human rationality involves activities such as being attentive to experience, interpreting and understanding experience, judging value and truth, and deciding how to translate into action what has been experienced, understood, and evaluated. An analysis of almost any meeting will reveal some involvement in these activities. The purpose of planning is to bring a group to an ordered approach to this basic, rational procedure.

Besides being an application of rational patterns, planning is also a decision-making tool. A decision is a choice from among alternatives. At a point of decision, persons are confronted with a situation in which they have some knowledge of what the *problem* is, what the possible *responses* to the problem are, and what the potential *consequences* of implementing certain responses are. However, most situations have a great deal of uncertainty about one or all of these aspects. Therefore, a formal decision-making method could be helpful as an aid to remove some of the uncertainty associated with choices. Action planning is anticipatory decision making. Choices are made for situations which have not yet occurred but might occur. The planning mindset implies that making commitments in advance and taking actions in the present influences future events and orients them in a desired direction to obtain desired results. Thus, uncertainty is superseded by creative human foresight and insight. A group doing planning and making choices develops a sense of potency through this type of organized application of human rationality. Although actual choices may fall short of the ideal, the artful application of the technology of rationality increases the quality of a community's response to its present history.

In order to explain planning it is helpful to separate the two components which are interwoven in real experience, namely, the conceptual framework and the sequence of human activities. What is called the methodology of action planning is the conceptual framework or guiding questions which are used in constructing a plan. The process aspect of action planning is the sequence of human activities used to arrive at the plan. A good approach to action planning is one in which both methodology and process are well developed and integrated.

The approach to action planning to be developed at length in this chapter has been given the shorthand designation DDAE.[1] DDAE is a systematic approach to planning which stimulates groups to:

- discuss and diagnose their problems
- formulate solutions to their problems
- take action to implement the solutions
- assess the effects of these actions.

DDAE emphasizes a methodology and process of planning with the further addition of a set of communication tools. Since no group in religious life works in isolation, the integration of a communication mandate facilitates the articulation of the working group with the larger community. DDAE is shorthand for *Dialogue*, *Decision*, *Action*, and *Evaluation*. These four words are the key to the methodology or concep-

---

[1] In a study of educational change by the Institute for the Development of Educational Activities, Inc. (I/D/E/A), the words Dialogue, Decision, Action, and Evaluation were used to characterize the essential processes of continuous renewal in schools. See Carmen M. Culver et al., *The Power to Change: Issues for the Innovative Educator*, *I/D/E/A Reports on Schooling* (New York: McGraw-Hill, 1973).

tual framework of the action planning outlined in this chapter.

- *Dialogue:* How does the group understand and value its situation?
- *Decision:* How will the group act in the future in addressing the particular issue at hand?
- *Action:* How is the implementation of action coordinated?
- *Evaluation:* What was learned from the action?

The process of DDAE is also built around the four key words. Each of the four words signifies a step in the process or sequence of human activities. Each step is a sequence in itself and will be treated separately. To enhance the self-contained feature of each step, the meeting format should be broken into four distinct sections. Figure 6.1 is a diagrammatic overview of each of the four processes.

The DDAE approach to action planning has a certain formality; but since it is oriented for group planning, flexibility is also present to adapt to the needs of any given group. Participation in decision making is important during this period of building religious life into the future. DDAE is ideally suited to group decision making in choice situations where the choice needs to be a quality one but where a high degree of uncertainty exists. Since the working group is composed of at least seven or eight members (including a leader) this process also helps to generate commitment of a number of people to the implementation of the decisions made. The end product of the DDAE process can be described as a program, i.e., a sequence of actions designed to obtain a specific result in a specific time period. Although the DDAE approach can be adapted to a long-range and comprehensive planning process, the orientation in this chapter is short-range (a week, a month, up to a year). During this period of breakdown, many communities are expanding efforts to explore and rebuild structures which have disintegrated. As a program-planning process for groups, DDAE has the potential to sig-

DECISION

· Clarifying Purpose
· Setting Goals
· Designing a Program Approach
· Determining Objectives
· Communicating the Decisions

DIALOGUE

· Orienting the Planning
· Generating Assumptions
· Assessing Needs
· Communicating the Dialogue

ACTION

· Designing the Projects
· Budgeting and Scheduling
· Implementing the Plan
· Communicating the Action

EVALUATION

· Establishing Criteria
· Measuring Performance
· Assessing Learning
· Communicating the Evaluation

FIGURE 6.1

nificantly increase a group's ability to cope with its own environment and to invent and construct desired structures for the future. DDAE should increase a group's capacity to learn, unlearn, and relearn. It develops a sense of potency and generates a sense of hope in the future.

Lest the realists rise up in revolt, it must be pointed out that there are limitations to DDAE. The previous chapters have already treated another whole dimension of coping with the present state of religious life, namely, that of the nonrational. In addition, some interpersonal skills are prerequisites for the effective use of DDAE. No amount of rational processing could overcome a lack of interpersonal skills: openness about feelings, acceptance of mistakes, facility to adapt to changing roles, allowance for others' feelings, ability to function under stress, and building of supporting relationships. Thus, while DDAE strengthens a group's ability to create desired futures, there are no automatic guarantees. DDAE cannot eradicate complexity or slow down the dynamic forces of change. It can only be one of serveral tools used to cope with the change and uncertainty of the present ambiguous state of religious life tottering between breakdown and revitalization.

Dialogue

When a group begins its planning work, the first thing it must do is explore the problem or issue at hand. This exploration includes some treatment of how the group understands and values its total situation. The process for achieving this end is called the dialogue process. If the meaning of dialogue is expanded, other words such as sharing, listening, appreciating, understanding, and communicating begin to enter in. Dialogue is the art of sharing experiences and reflections in order to reach a more complete and shared vision of the total situation. Dialogue is both the capacity to listen to others with the willingness to understand and the capacity to communicate with the intention of being understood. Since understanding is so subjective, it is important to realize that the meaning intended by a communicator is not necessarily the same as that received by the listener. Communication is given meaning by the receiver in the context of a personal framework of appreciation. Therefore a planning group must work at developing a common framework of appreciation, i.e., a common way of understanding and valuing the total situation. This process encourages the expression of diversity in unity by bringing the unique individual frameworks into a common vision.

The goal of the dialogue process is precisely the establishment of this common framework out of which to launch the treatment of the problem or issue at hand. There is a strong parallel to be found between this notion of framework and the phenomenon of myth or vision explained in the bias of foolishness. The expression of values and beliefs contributes dimensions of the underlying vision of the group to the shaping of attitudes and actions. Beliefs are surfaced about the situation a group is in, about the actions that should be taken, about the outcomes of possible actions, and about the range of actions open to a group. What needs to be done is to take the best information, both rational and nonrational, and draw from it an explicit framework which can be agreed to by the planning group.

In addition to the shared framework of appreciation, the dialogue process will also clarify the scope of the group's endeavor, the gathering and organizing of the planning information, and the identification of the problem and/or issue to be addressed. The work of this process can be described in four tasks. The first three tasks are the work of the dialogue meeting and the fourth is the communication of the results of this process.

Task 1: Orienting the Planning

This task consists of orienting the planning work. Orienting is a matter of developing a common set of expectations so that ambiguity and uncertainty about what the group is doing can be minimized. Unclear expectations among participants in a group are one of the main causes of unproductive planning. Expectations can be clarified when the answers to the following questions are developed:

Subject	• What is the problem or issue that brought this group together?
	• Do we agree it is important?
	• Are we committed to doing something about it?
Time Horizon	• When are the outcomes of the plan to be completed?
	• Is this time horizon realistic?
Role Clarification	• Leadership: Who will be providing leadership for the planning group?
	• Decisions: Who is responsible for making or approving the decisions in the plan?
	• Consultation: What persons or groups should be consulted in developing the plan?
	• Implementation: Who is responsible for implementing the plan?

These orienting questions help a group identify the main concern of its planning and the expectations which are common about the scope of its endeavor. When an actual group is at work, the most helpful approach to this phase involves discussion, consensus, and recording. The leader should attempt to facilitate discussion of the orienting questions that leads to consensus on a set of answers. The consensus answers are recorded for the group to see. An example of how one group (the government commission of the midwestern women's order) oriented its planning work is given in Table 6.1.

Task 2: Generating Assumptions

In any given group, each member has some information that is important to the planning process. Part of developing a shared framework of appreciation consists in making all the

---

TABLE 6.1: Orienting the Planning Work

Subject: Revision of the Province Government Plan
Time Horizon: December 1981
Role Clarification:

> Leadership: The Government Commission is responsible for constructing the revised plan under the leadership of its chairperson.

> Decisions: The revised plan must be submitted to the Provincial Chapter for final approval.

> Consultation: There should be input obtained from all the governmental bodies in the province (team, commissions, boards, . . .) and from all the sisters of the province.

> Implementation: The Government Commission will carry through the task of preparing a revised Province Government Plan to go to Rome.

---

available information explicit. Helpful information may range over such areas as data and facts about the present situation, feelings and intuitions about the present situation, constraints on potential action, and hopes and dreams which individuals have about future actions of the group. A group makes its information explicit by writing assumptions. Assumptions can contain "hard" information (objective data and facts) or "soft" information (subjective data and feelings). In order to facilitate the shared framework of appreciation, it is important to make as explicit as possible the "soft" data: beliefs, hopes, attitudes, values, fears, and doubts that individuals in the group have.

In generating assumptions the group leader should remind the group of the rationale for the activity. The technique can then be simply illustrated by sample assumptions about the planning group. The leader could use examples such as: "I assume that this group is eager to get on with the work they came for"; "I assume that some people are wondering where this activity will lead us"; and "I assume that there are some people in the group who do not know each other well." Then some time is provided for each member to list individual assumptions. One member of the group records assumptions requested from each member in turn until all are shared. It is helpful to make all this data visible so that continual scanning can promote synthesis and further assumptions. An example of some assumptions from the government commission's work is given in Table 6.2.

Task 3: Assessing Needs

Once the information is generated and collected, it must be evaluated. The group must attempt to cluster and focus the assumptions in order to pinpoint the important issues or

---

TABLE 6.2: Assumptions

I assume that
- we can build on the old government plan without starting completely over
- there is not much more than $300 available for this project
- many prefer to keep the team structure but with modifications
- we could learn from what other orders have tried in government
- the generalate will have some questions about the personal authority of the provincial
- sisters in the province have many opinions about our present structure
- the work the California province has done on religional coordinators might be useful
- we have to get started now if we are going to make the deadline

---

problems that require the group's attention. Care must be taken, on the one hand, that this clustering is not so broad and global that there is no clear-cut action indicated. On the other hand, there should not be so many issues or problems that the group can not do adequate focusing. A useful technique for recording the evaluation of all the information is to formulate need statements. These are statements which begin with the words "There is a need to" and finish by using a phrase to describe a problem or issue which requires the group's response.

In a working session, the need statements should again be generated on the individual level first and then on the group level. Each member tries to capture the major issues in one or two statements of need. Then a common list is obtained in round-robin fashion before the group moves on for review and further synthesis. After removing duplication and combining as much as seems needed, a reasonably compact list should result. The leader works with this last step until there is consensus on the list of needs. A partial list of the need statements of the government commission is given in Table 6.3.

Task 4: Communicating the Results of Dialogue

When the work of the dialogue phase is over, the group will move on to the next step. However, if anyone outside of the

---

TABLE 6.3: Need Statements

There is a need to prepare a Government Plan for presentation to the Provincial Chapter.

There is a need to get feedback from all sisters on ideas and feelings about government.

There is a need to dialogue with the Provincial Team on how their role has evolved over the last five years.

---

planning group is to be able to follow the development of the plan, there must be communication of the shared framework of appreciation that has been developed through the processing of all the information. Even the planning group itself will need to refer back in the course of the next phase. The best means of communicating the dialogue phase is the use of a dialogue paper. This consists of a printed reproduction of all the material in the charts for this process plus an explanation of the movement of the process. If the government commission sent a dialogue paper to the provincial team, it would be a combination of an introductory explanation plus the material in Tables 6.1, 6.2, and 6.3, i.e., orientation, assumptions, and need statements.

Decision

In the dialogue phase, a group develops a common perspective on the problems or issues which it must address in its planning for action to bring about desired results. It is important to note that actions and activities are only useful as a means to bring about some end result. It is a common failing for groups to concentrate on activities and neglect a clear discussion of the end to be accomplished by all the activities. Therefore, one of the key decisions to be made is that of the end result or goal. During the decision process the group will make three major decisions:

- *Why* do we want to address this issue? (*purpose*)

- *What* results do we want to accomplish by our actions? (*goal*)

- *How* will these results be accomplished? (*program approach and objectives*)

In the context of the revitalization of religious life, the notion of looking toward the future and creatively structuring action to bring about a desired future is very critical. The decisions to be made here have the potential to make a difference in the process of transformation from breakdown to revitalization.

The Vitality Curve of Chapter Three points out that the level of decision and action is part of the growth and breakdown cycle of any social group. The main work of the decision process will be described in four tasks. Again there is a further task of communicating the results of the group's effort in some concrete manner.

Task 1: Clarifying the Purpose

The accomplishment of a series of activities and certainly the achievement of an immediate goal can be very satisfying to a task-oriented group. However, that success is short-lived if there is not some deeper dimension to surface activities. There is a need for vision and motivating idealism to underlie a group's planning and activities. The first task of the decision process, then, is to clarify the purpose or unifying vision which acts as an imperative for the group's action. Statements of purpose express for the group the long-term outcomes toward which its efforts are directed. This unifying vision is an ideal which cannot be obtained within a specific time period nor in a measurable degree. But, in principle, it is reachable over a long time and therefore acts as a motivating factor. A statement of purpose should contain the description of several long-term outcomes which are the foci of the group's efforts. The language of the purpose statement should be clear and concise, yet inspirational. A helpful format for writing is to use an introductory phrase such as "The purpose of the _____ group is: (a) _____ , (b) _____ , (c) _____ ," filling in the major long-term outcomes which make up the purpose. The group leader needs to exercise some skill in striving for consensus in the large group on these points. It is interesting to note that the end which will be achieved farthest into the future comes first in the decision-making process. An example statement of purpose for the government commission is given in Table 6.4.

Task 2: Setting Goals

The planning now reaches the stage where the group turns its attention to the creation and invention of results that it would

---

TABLE 6.4: Statement of Purpose and Statement of Goal

I. The purpose of the Government Commission is
   a) to strive for the humanization of government structures in the province
   b) to promote a broad base of participation in province decision making
   c) to insure that province authority structures foster a balance of freedom and responsibility

II. Our goal is a condition in which we have developed a revised Ohio Province Government Plan which reflects the evolution in structure over the past five years and projects a dynamic structure to support our life and works into the near future.

---

like to achieve in the near future. In the model of community development, these results are intended to rebuild in the area of norms. This process can be described as the task of writing a goal statement. This goal statement must capture some of the hopes and dreams of the group and yet express them in practical action-oriented terms. The definition of the term "goal" as used here is intended to be focused and explicit. It is the description of the results or end state which the group hopes to experience when its action is complete. The goal is meant to describe a specific result which is obtainable in the time period set down by the group and under the present circumstances in which the group finds itself. The goal must be simultaneously realistic and challenging. The goal should elicit involvement from the group and excite the members to new realization.

To begin the process of writing a goal statement, it is good for the group leader to quickly review the need statements and statement of purpose. Then some time for individual consideration should be allowed. After each person has some individual idea of a goal statement, the group should break into small segments of three or four people and refine the individual statements into single statements for each small group. Then back in the large group setting, the process of synthesizing and refining can be facilitated to bring about the production of one goal statement which is acceptable to the whole group. It is helpful to write the statement with the phrase, "Our goal is a condition in which . . . ," followed by a description of the result which the group has now agreed to work toward together. The example of the goal statement for the government commission is given in Table 6.4.

If a planning group has enough time and patience, there is evidence to affirm theoretically that this is the best place to establish criteria for goal achievement. The activity consists of envisioning a state in which the newly developed goal has been successfully achieved. Through the use of completion statements such as "Our goal would be accomplished if we observed . . ." or "Our goal would be accomplished if people believed or felt . . ." some indicators of goal occurrence are listed. The purpose of this exercise is to capture, for later use, the group's thinking on the realistic expectations surrounding the goal. In concrete experience this activity is often put off until the evaluation process due to a pressure to accelerate toward action. The loss of effect due to delay of this activity does not seem to be of critical importance. A fuller development of this task is treated in the evaluation section later in this chapter.

Task 3: Designing a Program Approach

Even though the goal has been set now, the decision making is by no means finished. A simple analogy can illustrate. If someone sets a goal of a trip to Disneyland, there are a number of ways to accomplish that goal. One could fly, or a camper could be rented and driven across the country. There are a number of broad courses of action that would bring about the accomplishment of a trip to Disneyland. There are pros and cons to each different strategy and these must be weighed in order to make a wise decision. The determination of a basic approach or alternative for achieving the goal is the next area for decision making. The question being answered here is: "How is the group going to get to the desired goal?" The program approach is a broad course of action selected from among alternatives as the best way to obtain the goal in view of the assumptions and statement of purpose completed earlier.

In designing a program approach, the first practical task is to determine the criteria that will be used. The group looks over the assumptions, to review the framework from which they are operating. Then in small groups a list of "must" characteristics and a list of "want" characteristics are drawn up. "Must" characteristics are those which the program approach is required to have for it to be acceptable to the group. The "want" characteristics indicate what makes one strategy more desirable than the other. The small-group lists are then synthesized into single lists by the large group. It is helpful if these lists are compact and not too lengthy. The program approach criteria for the government commission are listed in Table 6.5.

TABLE 6.5: Program Approach Criteria

A. "Must" Criteria

1. Due to the travel distance involved, the total Commission cannot meet more than once a month.
2. Communication to the sisters of the province must be happening as the Plan is developing.

B. "Want" Criteria

1. It would be desirable to have a questionnaire done by a computer.
2. It would be desirable to have *every* sister provide input on the experience with the present plan and on the revised plan after it is developed.

Once the criteria have been determined, the group turns its attention to inventing different program approach alternatives. The group should first focus on the distinct elements or activities that could be used as part of a strategy. These can be obtained through brainstorming and outside research. The program approach elements are then arranged into alternative approaches. Through juggling and rearranging it should be possible to come up with two or three clearly identifiable alternatives which can be labeled alternatives A, B, etc. The group now moves on to comparison of the alternatives through application of the criteria. It is imporant to list the positive and negative consequences for the whole group to see. The actual choice of a program alternative should be one which satisfies all of the "must" criteria. Secondly, it should satisfy the "want" criteria better than any other alternative. While there will not be one perfect alternative, this process allows the group to make a fairly well-thought-out decision of one alternative over the other. Example program-approach alternatives for the government commission are given in Table 6.6.

Task 4: Determining Objectives

Once the broad course of action to get to the goal is decided, the next decision needed is that which determines the intermediate steps along the way to the goal. The term "objectives" is used to describe these major intermediate results. A key factor in motivating people to implement planning is a set of objectives which combine specific results with a challenge that will excite people and call for a commitment to accomplish them. Objectives should be specific and concrete enough to describe a single key result which can be measured and evaluated. Because of this concrete aspect, objectives must be attainable within the constraints and resources that limit the present situation of the given group. The planning group must understand and accept the objectives since they are going to play a large part in carrying them out. The written form of the objectives should be in the past tense, with a target date specified for each. The actual process of

---

TABLE 6.6: Program-Approach Alternatives

A. A Professional Consulting Group

1. Definition
   Management Group Z, Inc., would be asked to work with the Government Commission to develop the revised plan.

2. Negative Consequences
   a. The cost would be high.
   b. This group may not understand how to include our charism and religious values in the planning.

3. Positive Consequences
   a. This group guarantees satisfactory results.
   b. We would have professional input on the structuring of social organizations.

B. Government Commission

1. The Government Commission would use their own and other resources within the province to develop a revised plan.

2. Negative Consequences
   a. The plan may have a narrow scope due to a kind of "inbred" thinking.
   b. Since the members of the Government Commission all have full-time jobs, they may have very little time to devote to the planning.

3. Positive Consequences
   a. The province will feel more secure about a plan developed by us.
   b. We would become experienced in applying some planning techniques.

---

writing should be done in the small-group/large-group progression that has been used throughout. It is helpful in each situation to list the key results first and then to go back over these to put target dates on each with a view to the overall progression in time. The finished product then will be a concise list of the key steps to the goal, in a time frame that is realistic and attainable in view of the horizon set back at the beginning. The grammar of objectives could be diagrammed this way: subject/constraint/past-tense verb/target date. Some examples of this form for objectives are given in Table 6.7 from the government commission.

Task 5: Communicating Decisions

The decisions of this phase of the planning work are preserved and made available to others outside the group through a decision paper. It is important to have the completed decisions in a handy form for use as reference throughout the action phase. The decisions are the guidelines and the stimuli for action. Since the work of the group throughout this phase has been done on blackboard or newsprint for large group viewing, it is easy to summarize. A decision paper would then consist of the material on purpose, goal, program approach, and objectives. A decision paper for the government commission would be a compilation of Tables 6.4, 6.5, 6.6, and 6.7 along with an explanation of how the group moved through those tasks.

TABLE 6.7: Objectives

A. A mechanism to obtain feedback from all sisters of the province is completed and analyzed by April 1980.
B. An investigation into the government structures of at least six other orders is completed by December 1980.
C. A rough draft of the Plan is evaluated by sisters of the province by May 1981.

Action

Action is the very center of action planning. All of the planning work is done in an effort to bring about meaningful action. It cannot be said often enough that the renewal of structures and operational systems by religious communities is undoubtedly a worthy target for meaningful action. It is at this stage that the work moves out of the group setting into a context of individual effort. It is therefore important that the participants in the group and in the action have developed a commitment to the action that is going to be done. Once some further initial planning is done, individuals will be responsible for organizing and carrying out particular parts of the action. Without a vision of where and why the parts fit into the whole, the action will not lead to the corporate goal. So, the importance of involvement in and commitment to the previous phases cannot be underestimated for the successful achievement of this phase. There are four tasks used to describe the work of this step. The first two tasks are a continuation of the mode of planning and prethinking. The third task is the actual implementation of action. The last task is again one of communication of the activities of this phase.

Task 1: Designing the Projects

The goal is the desired end result of the process of planning and creating. In order to orient the human effort needed to achieve a goal, the major steps along the road to the goal are outlined in the form of objectives. Now a further breakdown is used to delineate the activities needed to accomplish each intermediate step or objective. This process is called designing the projects. Every objective needs to be looked at in order to determine what activities will be required to attain it. Upon examination, it may be found that some objectives will only require routine activities. The projects used to reach these objectives can then be described as routine projects. There is no need to design these projects, since efficient methods are already known and have already been used. An example of an objective requiring routine activities would be

C in Table 6.7. This objective would actually involve two activities: the writing of a rough draft and the channeling of this draft through established patterns for province evaluation. Since both of these activities are familiar to the participants in the group, there is no need to design a project for this objective. The only further attention that it needs will be looked at in Task 2 of this phase.

There are, however, objectives which require innovative planning. When the method for obtaining an objective is untried or uncertain, care is needed in the design of such a nonroutine project. The attention needed at this stage can be compared to that which was pointed out during the consideration of program approach. Judgments are called for concerning the requirements ("must" aspect) of the project and the desirable characteristics ("want" aspect) of the project. Alternatives are again generated, with an evaluation based on positive and negative consequences to follow. A decision is then made as to which of the alternative projects is the best selection for the attainment of the relevant objective. The actual work on this process will probably not be as detailed as it was in the program-approach phase. Probably even the size of the group doing the work could be reduced. It is feasible to subdivide the objectives and distribute them among small segments of the total group for the designing of projects. For this activity, this increase in efficiency should not decrease effectiveness. A project for one objective of the government commission is defined in Table 6.8.

TABLE 6.8: An Action Paper

Area: Government
Project Manager: Chairperson of the Government Commission

I. *Objective:* A mechanism to obtain feedback from all sisters of the province is completed and analyzed by April 1980.

Table 6.8—Continued

II. *Project Definition:* The Government Commission will ask Sister Mary X to act as a consultant in the preparation, administration, and analysis of a province-wide questionnaire. The questionnaire will be concerned with attitudes and ideas about government over the past five years and into the next several years. The analysis should yield a picture of present thinking on present structure and new ideas and trends.

III. *Project Budget:*
   A. Human Effort

Sister Mary X	3 person-days =	3
Government Commission Subcommittee (3)	$^1/_2$ person-days =	$1^1/_2$
Government Commission (10)	$^1/_2$ person-days =	5
Sisters of province (480)	$^1/_{24}$ person-days =	20
		29$^1/_2$ person-days

   B. Finances

Computer compilation and printout	$150.00
Postage	6.00
Paper, stencils	7.50
Travel	35.00
	$198.50

IV. *Project Schedule:*

Event	Date
Government Commission lists areas to be covered in questionnaire	October 21, 1979
Sr. Mary X draws up rough draft for Commission	November 15, 1979
Government Commission approves final draft for publication	December 15, 1979
Completed questionnaires sent to computer	February 1, 1980

Task 2: Budgeting and Scheduling

After bringing the planning work to this point, only two details are left to be worked through. The unfinished dimensions are budgeting and scheduling. Budgeting is the determination and assignment of resources required to reach each objective. A good sense of budget provides for maximum utilization of the available resources. A budget is worked out for each project first and then a sum is obtained for each objective. Then, by adding, a total budget for the whole plan can be set up. Budgeting involves more than just financial resources, materials, and facilities. As a matter of fact, those are probably the simplest to budget. Much more challenging is the budgeting of human effort and time. The budgeting of human effort is expressed in terms of person-hours. It is helpful to be reminded of the tendency to be unrealistic in this area. (After an initial estimate is made of person-hours for some job, it is usually realistic to double that amount!)

The remaining detail is the job of establishing the time requirements for projects. This task requires not only a perspective on the immediate objective and its projects, but also a perspective on the overall work flow and timing. Coordination and a good spread of the work over the available time should be the goal of this task. The schedulers should be careful not to overburden any people or any time periods. The actual work of budgeting and scheduling can be delegated into very small working groups. An example of the budgeting and scheduling of a government-commission objective is given in Table 6.8.

A second approach to scheduling is also worth mentioning. The overall effort of the plan is the focus, and the process is one of setting up milestones. Milestones are deadlines chosen for the completion of each significant amount or type of effort. They are indicators of any or all of the following:

- *decision point*   "go" or "no go" to the next
                            step

- *learning point*   reassessment of direction
                            based on feedback

- *feedback point*   seeking response on progress of plan

- *action point*   meetings scheduled, activity begun, etc.

- *evaluation point*   review by outside experts

- *communication point*   publication date

If a group used the milestone approach to comprehensive scheduling, it would have to select the milestones and assign the time frame in a large-group setting. This approach does provide an easy reference for evaluation by those implementing the action plans.

Task 3: Implementing the Plan

In developing an action plan a group has worked out a complex of interrelated activities that must be accomplished if the desired goal is to be reached. Once all this groundwork has been laid, it is not necessary for everyone in the group to participate in all of the action. In fact, the reason for organizing groups is so that there is a division of labor. Thus delegation of work and responsibility is now needed. If such delegation is to work effectively, then the person or subgroup accepting the delegation must clearly understand what is to be done, when it is to be done, and how to report on the progress toward the final results (results, timing, system of reporting). Because there are people to whom separate parts of the plan are delegated, there must be some one person who is responsible for the overall coordination and monitoring of the action. This person concentrates on unification of the diverse activities into a thrust for the common goal. If actual performance in any sector begins to deviate from the expected, then corrective action must be initiated by the coordinator. This should not be seen as negative but as normal and constructive in the course of human activity.

In implementing a plan of action, there are almost always unforeseen problems, difficulties, and circumstances. Some common problems are: not including all the results that are needed to attain the goal; the occurrence of an unforeseen barrier to achievement of the goal; unforeseen and disruptive consequences of some actions; and unrealistic time constraints. When a problem of some import surfaces, the action called for is review and replanning of the relevant portion of the plan. Sometimes replanning might mean adjustment of a minor portion of the total plan; sometimes it might demand that the rest of the plan from the problem point onward be reworked entirely. Even though this may be a difficult reality to cope with, put into the context of goal achievement it must be seen as worthwhile. While this whole rational approach is an invaluable tool, it lays no claim to infallibility.

Task 4: Communicating the Results of Action

While actions may speak for themselves, the project designs, budgets, and schedules need to be printed for reference and for communication to others outside of the planning group. An action paper like that in Table 6.8 could be published for each objective as a means of communicating the work of the action phase. And, of course, should there be a need for some replanning of any significant amount, the results of this should be published for communication purposes. The action papers will provide a point of departure for the next step which is evaluation.

Evaluation

Having experienced extensive analysis and planning, the members of a planning group will reach some point where reflection over the whole proceeding can occur. This point will be at or near the completion of the action phase. The purpose of looking back over the whole process is to learn from the unfolding that has occurred and to build the competence of the group for future planning situations. Some important questions to ask in this evaluation process are:

- Was our goal accomplished?
- What was the impact of our group action?
- What have we learned?

The methodologies for evaluation can be clustered into two groups: goal-oriented evaluation and goal-free evaluation. In goal-free evaluation, the group considers some general questions in reflecting on the experiences that have occurred. Some sample general questions are: What are the consequences of our planned action? Why did things happen the way they did? What can we learn from the experiences? In goal-oriented evaluation, the actual results are measured against the expected or planned results. The group devises some way to measure the actual accomplishment and then compares that to the ideal conditions that were envisioned during the planning stages. From an analysis of the gap between the real and the ideal, areas of weakness will be discovered as well as some answers to the general questions mentioned above. A planning group must learn from such mistakes as blind spots, incorrect assumptions, unclear needs, overambitious goals, poor communication, and inadequate execution of action. Concurrently, there is the need to discover and capitalize on strong points in future planning.

The material presented here will be concerned with goal-oriented evaluation. The process will be described in three tasks along with the presentation of the fourth task of communication.

Task 1: Establishing Performance Criteria

Since the goal is the focus of all the planning activity, it is also the place to begin the evaluation process. The group must review the goal-setting process in order to regain the intent and the framework of the stated goal. From this reorientation, then, some realistic expectations for goal occurrence can be listed. As was mentioned previously, this task can be completed in the decision process. If this is the case, then the criteria developed there are simply used here in the evaluation process.

A good way for a group to generate performance criteria is to complete the following statements:

• Our goal would be accomplished if we observed . . .

- Our goal would be accomplished if people believed or felt . . .

Performance criteria should be stated in observable terms, in terms of things that can be seen and measured. Later, when other people are consulted for feedback on their perceptions, the data obtained will only be as concrete as the criteria are concrete. It is almost always possible for a group to generate more performance criteria than it could ever reasonably expect to measure. Therefore, once a large list is drawn up from the whole group, a selection process can be used. The group should select the criteria which it believes to be the most significant and the most practical to measure. These criteria will then serve as a standard against which to measure the actual accomplishment of the goal. Some sample performance criteria for the government-commission goal are given in Table 6.9.

TABLE 6.9: An Evaluation Paper

I. Goal

Our goal is a condition in which we have developed a revised Ohio Province Government Plan which reflects the evolution in structure over the past five years and projects a dynamic structure to support our life and works into the near future.

II. Performance Criteria

Our goal would be accomplished if we observed:

1. province government structures with flexibility and adaptive capability built in;

2. a clearer understanding of the provincial's role on the team;

3. passage of the revised plan at the Provincial and General Chapters.

Table 6.9—Continued

Our goal would be accomplished if people felt:

4. more comfortable with the decentralization of province authority;

5. that their input on the government questionnaire had been used in revising the 1969 Government Plan.

III. Sample Questionnaire Data

285 sisters answered the questionnaire, 2 more sent written comments only, and 215 did not answer at all. About 20% of the answerers can be described as very involved in province government; another 55% are very interested participants in an indirect manner; 17% are not so active but try to be informed.

Should more decisions be made provincially than locally?

33% yes   49% no   18% uncertain

Should the provincial assembly have the power to change the Province Government Plan as needed?

41% yes   28% no   31% uncertain

In the comments section, 179 sisters or 62% of the respondents took the opportunity to expand on their feedback. The 179 commenters represent 37% of the total province. Concerning the 1976 preparation questionnaire, a request was made for feeling about the use of the data from that in the revision of the Government Plan. A large number of unqualified favorable comments were given; negative comments centered around the difficulty of using data spread over a continuum of opinion; a small number of comments expressed a rather strong desire to have no more time and energy spent on government plans.

Table 6.9—Continued

IV. Some Strengths and Weaknesses
    Strengths
    • there was good grass-roots participation in the whole revision process

    • the assumptions about opinion concerning team structure were mostly true

    • the coordination and delegation of tasks went smoothly

    Weaknesses
    • since the plan was approved by the General Chapter, there has not been enough effort at orienting the whole province to the new aspects

    • our projection of structure was probably short-sighted since we have the team-contact problem already

V. Some Recommendations
    1. In the dialogue phase, the listing of assumptions could have explored the future more thoroughly so that a more creative need statement could have been formulated in this area.

    2. If the structures which other orders have devised are used as a resource again, there should be personal contact in addition to written contact.

Task 2: Measuring Performance

Once the group has decided on standards for judging performance, it must go out and gather data from people who have some perspective from which to make a judgment about the performance of the planning group. Two effective means of getting feedback on performance are the use of questionnaires and interviews. The performance criteria developed in the preceding step are the backbone for the questions used in the instrument to be developed for measuring performance. Whatever the instrument, it is very important to make effective use of the data obtained and communicate the results. (Too many people have become weary of questionnaires whose results exist only to be neatly filed away into oblivion.) Once obtained, the raw data need to be organized and summarized into some usable form. This could probably best be done by one, two, or three people. Some data from the government-commission evaluation questionnaire are given in Table 6.9.

Task 3: Assessing Learning

After the results of the measuring instrument are collected, the group is ready to move into the heart of the evaluation process. With an overview of the feedback before them, the group can begin to pinpoint the strengths and weaknesses of its action. A good procedure here would be to list, for all to see, these strengths and weaknesses. Then the group could proceed with a reflective discussion about the "whys" of each point listed. This exploration is the key learning point in evaluation. An understanding of these "whys" leads to new insights about how to plan action in the future. These understandings can be captured on paper by drawing up a list of recommendations for future planning.

Task 4: Communicating Evaluation

Some summary of the evaluation process is needed for communication with others outside of the planning group, as well as for future reference for members of the group itself. A summary of the learning discovered during this cycle of human action could serve as a good starting point for a new action-planning cycle. The evaluation paper should contain a restatement of the goal, a list of the performance criteria, a summary of the data from the feedback instrument, the list of the strengths and weaknesses, and the list of recommendations for future planning. A sample action paper from the government commission is given in Table 6.9.

Conclusion

Since DDAE is more than a conceptual construct, its presentation is of little value without application. Efficient use of this methodology will require practice and skill development. To facilitate the utilization of DDAE, some further development of guidelines for use will be pursued. Some questions of "how," "when," and "who" still remain for clarification.

While DDAE is a highly structured process, the people and groups using it are not. The surroundings and the individuals are in a constant state of change. Hence, a flexible and organic planning structure is needed. The sequence of steps in DDAE should not be viewed rigidly. Neither is every step or task essential to the completion of all planning experiences. The structures outlined in this chapter are meant to serve as a guide. By adapting the structures and processes of meetings to the specific circumstances and demands of the working group, flexibility and productivity will be maintained. Experience is probably the only effective teacher of an organic approach. Personal and group skills in matching the process to the needs of the group will increase with each attempt to implement DDAE.

Which situations call for the use of DDAE? Since DDAE is an arduous and complex methodology, its use requires some qualifying conditions. Past experience has suggested the following factors as sources of qualification:

- seriousness of the situation
- dispersal of information
- complexity of a decision
- acceptability of a decision
- degree of conflict

If decisions are simple, clear-cut, and noncontroversial, then the time of the group should not be wasted on structuring such decisions. If, however, more than one person is needed to contribute information, to commit energy and effort, to balance ideologies, to improve quality, and to merge conflicting viewpoints, then it would be appropriate to engage a group in DDAE.

Selection of the people who will participate in the planning is another important aspect of application. The components of size and composition are particularly crucial. Experience has indicated that the largest group that should be used for DDAE is eight persons—including the leader. Groups larger than eight do not allow for sufficient participation by all. If there is a need to involve more than eight people, the group is simply subdivided into smaller, parallel, working clusters. Muliple working clusters demand that the leader be alert to provide times for synthesizing.

Criteria for the actual selection of individuals are almost as broad as the range of planning issues. However, three key questions can serve as guidelines: Who has information and ideas needed in addressing the problem at hand? Who has responsibility for the area in which the problem lies? Who will be concerned with implementation of the action? The effect of composition on the selection process is ambiguous. The pros and cons of homogeneous versus heterogeneous arrangements have not been settled. With homogeneity, some creativity and cross-fertilization is lost; with heterogeneity, the possibilities for conflict and barriers to interpersonal exchange are heightened. Therefore, the only answer to the question of composition is balance, i.e., a balance of people to maximize the balance of positive and negative consequences of homogeneous and heterogeneous groupings.

One more "who" concern is that of the selection of the leader of the planning group. Some practical prerequisites concerning ability to organize and lead a meeting are taken for granted. Further dimensions of leadership style grow out of the recent attention to process. The person chosen to be the leader will have to be attentive to process much more than content. As a result, it is better that the leader not have a large personal stake in the content of the planning. The dimensions of process that the leader must especially facilitate in DDAE are interpersonal communication and guidance of the work flow. To be successful as a planning team, each member of the group must experience support, listening, explanation, and consideration. Furthermore, the group must perceive that the interactions are organized and moving toward some achievement of order and meaning for the present situation. The selection of a leader or facilitator is a key to successful application of DDAE.

If a group takes seriously the challenge of learning to plan, then it is inevitable that obstacles and perplexities will occur along the way. There is no magical solution, of course, but only the promise of slowly increasing competence that comes with persevering effort. This perseverence could be called planning to learn!

In the final analysis, the renewal of religious life will not be the result of self-sufficient human effort. Despite the technological possibilities of collective brain power and its application, there is a stronger force which animates revitalization, namely, the dynamic presence of the Lord. An individual and communal sensitivity to this dimension must surely guide our course into the future.

Chapter Seven

Exploring the Relationship of Charism, the Founder and the Vitality Curve

> It is for the good of the Church that institutes have their own proper character and functions. Therefore, the spirit and aims of each founder should be faithfully accepted and retained, as indeed should each institute's sound traditions, for all of these constitute the patrimony of the institute. (*Perfectae Caritatis*, 2)

In order to be faithful to the teaching of the Council, must not "the members of each community who are seeking God above all else, combine contemplation with apostolic love? . . ." Only in this way will you be able to reawaken hearts to truth and divine love in accordance with the charisms of your founders who were raised up by God within His Church. Thus the Council rightly insists on the obligation of religious to be faithful to the spirit of their founders, to their Evangelical intentions, and to the example of their sanctity. In this it finds one of the principles for the present renewal and one of the most secure criteria for judging what each institute should undertake. In reality, the charism of the religious life . . . is the fruit of the Holy Spirit who is always at work within the Church. . . . It is precisely here that the dynamism proper to each religious family finds its origin. . . . The interior impulse which is the response to God's call stirs up in the depth of one's being certain fundamental options. Fidelity to the exigencies of these fundamental options is the touchstone of authenticity in religious life. . . . The variety of forms which give each institute its own individual character . . . have their root in the fullness of the grace of Christ. (*Evangelica Testificatio*, 10–12)

Three main sources for the genuine renewal of religious life indicated by the documents of the Second Vatican Council are the gospel, the signs of the times, and the spirit of the founder. Serious research and reflection on the last-mentioned source, the spirit of the founder, has been undertaken by most congregations only within the past five or six years. The reasons for this can be traced to a number of attitudes. Perhaps at first the words "spirit of the founder" seemed deceptively simple, and it was assumed that as adaptations proceeded the return to the original spirit of the institute would automatically follow. Perhaps, too, there was the hidden assumption that the spirit of the institute was something everybody knew and took for granted. For some others there may have been a resistance, conscious and unconscious, to returning to *anything*, even the spirit of the founder, for fear that renewal might be replaced by simple antiquarianism.

While at first the spirit of the founder looks like an interesting workshop topic, and even an inspirational one, most congregations found that these initial forays into the history and development of their religious families laid open the complexities as well as the riches of such a search. Chapter Four indicated the essential relationship between revitalization and the recovering of the founder's charism. Part 1 of this chapter will provide some useful guidelines for this recovery process by suggesting some clarifications about the nature of charism and then by pointing to some mistakes that should be avoided in the process. Part 2 will analyze some effects of the stages of the Vitality Curve on the concept of charism. Part 3 will raise some exploratory questions concerning the founding charism. Part 4 will discuss the importance and use of foundational texts. Finally, some metaphors or models which, by promoting a different self-understanding for a religious congregation, can support the task of recovery and exploration will be suggested in Part 5.

Part 1: Principles and Pitfalls

The nature and function of charisms is a relatively underdeveloped area of theological investigation. True, the writings of St. Paul acknowledge the variety of gifts present in the early Christian community and the tensions produced by them. After St. Jerome translated the word *charismata* in the New Testament in every case but one as *dona*, however, the term itself seems to have had little attention until modern times. The one exception of St. Jerome was in translating 1 Cor. 12:31, where the word's context gives the impression that charisms have to do only with the miraculous or extraordinary. Subsequent history corroborated this understanding. From approximately the second century, the alarm which followed upon the Montanist heresy encouraged the view that the charismatic gifts were given only to the early Church in order to facilitate the first stages of its life. The events of the Reformation period moved Catholic ecclesiology to concern itself almost exclusively with institutional factors in the Church's life.[1] Consequently, a rather false dichotomy was construed between the "official" and the "charismatic" church, causing an unhealthy tension between prophetic and priestly elements and identifying the former with renewal and the latter with formalism and ritualism. This tension was

---

[1] Karl Rahner, "Observations on the Factor of the Charismatic in the Church," in *Theological Investigations,* vol. 12 (New York: Seabury Press, 1974), pp. 81–97. See also Rahner's *The Dynamic Element in the Church* (London: Burnes and Oates, 1964). Edward D. O'Connor points out that "when the New Testament was translated into Latin, the term *charisma* almost disappeared, being usually translated by *gratia, donum,* or *donatio.* But St. Jerome retained the Greek term in 1 Corinthians 12:31, 'Aemulamini autem charismata meliora,' where its connection with the list just given by St. Paul would naturally tend to confirm the connection between charism and the marvelous in Latin thought" ("The New Theology of Charisms in the Church," *American Ecclesiastical Review* 161 (September 1969) 145–59). O'Connor's article traces the history of the word "charism" and its disappearance from Catholic theology.

felt more acutely in the Roman Catholic tradition because of its heavy structuralization and its increasing insistence on the principles of authority and the advantages of centralization.[2] The classical view of charism, nevertheless, which identified the charismatic with the marvelous and miraculous, prevailed throughout the Christian church up until modern times.

In 1943 Pius XII, in *Mystici Corporis,* affirmed the validity of the charismatic elements in the Church as balancing the hierarchic elements, without, however, elaborating much on the gifts and functions of all the members. A little more than twenty years later the documents of the Second Vatican Council contain fourteen passages in which the word *charisma* or "charismatic" appear. Still, though, little is said about the interplay of charismatic and institutional elements in the everyday life of the Church.[3] Although Karl Rahner, Yves Congar, Hans Küng, and other theologians have made substantial contributions to the explication of the theology of charism, a comprehensive study remains to be done.[4] Still it is possible to draw from the theological work already completed some basic principles by which to guide the process of recovering the charism and spirit of the founder as well as the charism of the present-day congregation.

The methodology used here, that of treating the subject of the charism of religious life or of the founder within the context of the general theology of charism, is suggested by the approach of the Vatican II documents, where religious life is treated first in *Lumen Gentium* before it is given specific

---

[2] R. Aubert, "Preface," *Concilium 37: Prophets in the Church* (New York: Paulist Press, 1968), pp. 2–3. Gabriel Moran presents some insightful questions on the validity of the term "centralization" in *Religious Body: Design for a New Reformation* (New York: Seabury Press, 1974), pp. 200ff.

[3] Rahner, "Observations on the Factor of the Charismatic in the Church," p. 85.

[4] See Rahner's article (n. 1) for bibliographical references on the topic. Another useful contribution to the discussion is *Theological and Pastoral Orientations in the Catholic Charismatic Renewal* (Malines Document), available from the Communication Center, P.O. Drawer A, Notre Dame, Indiana 46556.

attention in *Perfectae Caritatis*. The method to be used in this chapter will be to clarify particular principles concerning charism according to our current theological understanding, and then to indicate how the principle, if ignored, misunderstood, or misinterpreted, is in danger of becoming an impediment to the discovery-recovery process.

The first two principles to be considered are closely related. They are: 1) that charisms are present universally in the Church, and 2) that charisms are frequently gifts of quite an ordinary nature. A concentration on structure and institution in the Church and the association of charism with what is spectacular or miraculous (speaking in tongues, miracles of healing, etc.) have clouded if not prevented the valuing of numerous gifts granted for the building up of the Body of Christ. Passages from Ephesians (4:1–16), 1 Corinthians (12, 13, 14), and Romans (12:1–8, 16:1) suffice to illustrate that: 1) the gifts of the Spirit include what later came to be separated out as "offices"; 2) the well-being and maturity of the Body depend on the proper functioning of diverse parts; 3) while some gifts are unusual (e.g., glossolalia), most of them are indeed quite in the order of everyday tasks. It is significant that 1 Corinthians 13, the famous explication of love, is placed between the chapters in which Paul speaks of the other gifts (12, 14), and he introduces this paean to charity by saying, "Now I will show you the way which surpasses all the others." As Cardinal Suenens, addressing the Second Vatican Council, emphasized, "Thus, to St. Paul the Church of the living Christ does not appear as some kind of administrative organization, but as a living web of gifts, of charisms, of ministries."[5]

These two principles which give a fuller interpretation to the meaning of charism give a sound perspective from which to view the gift in general of religious life in the Church or the more specific gift of a given congregation. Much research

---

[5] Cardinal Leon-Joseph Suenens, "The Charismatic Dimension of the Church," in *Council Speeches of Vatican II*, ed. Y. Congar, H. Küng, and D. O'Hanlon (London/New York, 1964), pp. 18–21.

into the history of the founding of a congregation can prove not only fruitless but even frustrating, if there is a straining to find something terribly unique, special, extraordinary. The essential task for the congregation is to explore its own reality, to reflect on its own particular complex of gifts. This exercise of research and reflection should be done not in order to highlight its superiority over other groups, but rather with a view to becoming more conscious of its own gifts so that they can be more properly anointed and placed at the service of the Church. Rediscovering the particular charism of the congregation should not be motivated by a sense of competition with other congregations, for this would result in completely obstructing the action of the Spirit in the total Body, which is the Church. The variety of charisms, as pointed out by Hans Küng, demands precisely the opposite of an emphasis on superiority, differences, or competition. "These charismata, whether they be the more outstanding or the more simple and widely diffused, are to be received with thanksgiving and consolation for they are especially suited to and useful for, the needs of the Church."[6]

A characteristic of a healthy self-image is the understanding, acceptance, and appreciation of one's gifts precisely because they are one's own and not especially because they are different from someone else's. Difference is certainly acknowledged. But the person who needs always to emphasize his or her difference from others may only succeed in appearing peculiar. Religious congregations should keep this in mind as they try to discover their own uniqueness of charism, lest uniqueness become more important than the understanding, acceptance, and appreciation of the particular graced reality that is the congregation.[7]

---

[6] Hans Küng, "The Charismatic Structure of the Church," *Concilium* 4 (1965) 46ff.

[7] An article by Philip Kaufman, O.S.B., "The One and the Many: Corporate Personality," provides some interesting insight for a possible consideration of religious community as a corporate personality (*Worship* 42 (November 1968) 546–56).

A third important principle is the understanding of charism as gift and call, that is, that charism has an apostolic nature. The word apostolic here should not be construed as meaning only activity. Since the word takes its meaning from the Greek, "to send," it implies a recipient of what or whom is sent. The apostolic nature of charism means, then, a gift and call to become someone and/or to do something on behalf of others. The exercise of the charism is directed toward the building up of the Kingdom and not merely toward self-development.

Specifying charism in this way distinguishes it from a talent which might be developed solely for the good of the individual possessing it. Charisms, then, are powers turned outward toward others rather than toward self-fulfillment alone.When charisms are effective, it might be said they are a sign that the Kingdom of God has come. As a gift that is a call to service, charism contains within it the ability to perform that service. Furthermore, these gifts to the individual are effective for the building up of the Kingdom by being anointed, as it were, by the community. In other words, the exercise of the charism is relational.[8]

This dimension of the charism is an important criterion directing a congregation's search into that particular gift for service which is incarnated in the congregation. The relational aspect of charism pertains not simply to the individual within the congregation but to the congregation within the Church as well. This principle of "being or doing on behalf of others" provides a norm for discerning which of the numerous gifts and talents given to its members the congregation is seriously responsible for developing. Without doubt, there are obligations in the order of personal affirmation and charity toward the individual members on the part of the congregation as an entity. It is essential, however, that the order of

---

[8] See: W. Koupal's "Charism: A Relational Concept," *Worship* 42 (November 1968) 539–45; "Charism" in the *Encyclopedia of Theology* (ed. Karl Rahner), where Rahner speaks of charism as an assistance to ministry. "Apostolic Charism" by Robert J. Nogosek (*Lumen Vitae* 25 (March 1970) 132–38) is also helpful in elaborating this point.

personal affirmation does not subsume the order of apostolic service which gives the institute its *raison d'être*. Neither should the congregation see revitalization simply as a preservation of its own life without reference to the needs of the Church and the world.

The fourth and final principle to be kept in mind is that while charisms are a permanent element in the nature of the Church, they constantly appear, nevertheless, in new forms. It is in this way that the Holy Spirit continually renews the Church and equips it to serve the ever-changing needs of the world. There is, therefore, a constant need for rediscovery of charisms, since their manifestation will be conditioned by the needs of the Church at a given time in history. Contained in this principle is the assumption that charism will be characterized by variety.

Several implications for revitalization result from this principle. First, it requires prayerful discernment by the congregation to distinguish institutional forms from the charism they were developed to make effective. Since charism implies a gift and call, it is imperative that the call not be mistaken for an internal echo. The signs of the times, the third basis for renewal indicated in *Perfectae Caritatis*, will serve to prevent this mistaken identity of charism with familiar institutional forms. This does not mean that older institutional forms are absolutely *passé*. It should not be assumed, however, that they are *au courant* without a serious effort to evaluate their competence to make an effective response to the contemporary needs of the world.

This brief exposition about the nature of charism is not intended to provide a simplistic view of revitalization. Rootedness, that is, having a past, having a history, can also be experienced as a burden of givenness when a congregation views its members increasing in age and diminishing in numbers. The institutionalized insights of the past now literally concretized in buildings and groups and personnel and programs, and whose management requires such constant and immediate action, can paralyze a congregation and prevent it from asking deep and painful questions. The following section suggests a way of viewing the life cycle of a congregation so that its history can be a source of learning and not a reason for bleak resignation.

Part 2: The Life Cycle of the Charism

Since, for all practical purposes, the word charism disappeared from the working vocabulary of theology at a very early period, it is not surprising that it fails to appear in the words of the founders of religious institutes or in foundational texts. The growth in understanding of this element in the life of the Church, however, enables us to use it as a focal point from which to view the history of religious congregations in general. Specific differences can be inserted as each congregation applies this focus to its own history.

The two dimensions of charism, gift and call, each connote a slightly different experience in the one who receives it. "Gift" implies something pleasing, acceptable, eagerly anticipated, perhaps. On the other hand, the word "call" can sometimes connote the idea of an intrusion, something unexpected. Scripture alone is enough to reinforce the concept that the call, when it is from God, has often meant a challenge and risk for the one called. Likewise, in the case of major founders, it is not too difficult to see them in the role of prophets, that is, persons who are particularly sensitive to historical change and endowed with a gift for interpreting the signs of the times. These sensitivities, which give an acute understanding of both new needs and new opportunities, often engage the founder in an opposition to what has become established, familiar, or comfortable in the institution or in society.

The spontaneity of nature and grace brings about a certain dynamism in the life of the Church which produces, especially at times of crisis, prophetic persons who are able to disentangle the gospel from the institutional maze which prevents it from being heard. Very often this prophetic vision is implemented in the establishment of a religious order.[9] At the time of foundation, the response to the call is in a certain sense undifferentiated; that is, there is a wholeheartedness of response that frequently is expressed in a universal language similar to the "Fiat" or "Do whatever he tells you" which scripture records as Mary's response. The founder is supported in his or her life and witness by a small group that can identify with the founder's response. In this early period of organization, the style of life is usually seen to be dictated more by a spontaneous response to this charismatic leader than by rigid structures. The apostolic expressions for the multiple gifts possessed by the first followers is characterized by a certain spontaneity and freedom, secured by the strong presence of the founder and the vision which is shared. Such foundations take on the character of movements which can be said to be both the cause and the effect of social change. This founding community is then "organized for, ideologically motivated by, and committed to a purpose which implements some form of personal and social change."[10] The center, or central zone, for the group is not a spatially located phenomenon. It is a phenomenon in the realm of values, beliefs, and symbols. "The central zone partakes of the nature of the sacred. It is the center because it is the ultimate and irreducible; and it is felt to be such by many who cannot give explicit articulation to that irreducibility."[11] Thus the foundational or pioneer period generates a sense of the possible, and great resources of physical, psychic, and spiritual energy seem available.

While the primary goal of the new group is not to recruit, still the existence of the new society and the work they begin to do almost of themselves attract new members. This influx

---

[9] See *Concilium* 37: *Prophets in the Church*.

[10] Luther P. Gerlach and Virginia H. Hine, *People, Power, Change: Movements of Social Transformation* (Indianapolis: Bobbs-Merrill, 1970), p. xvi.

[11] Max Weber, *On Charisma and Institution Building*, ed. S. N. Eisenstadt (Chicago: University of Chicago Press, 1968), p. xxix.

of new members, added to the geographical dispersion characteristic of the expansion period, makes it imperative that the initial vision and spirit be somehow preserved. The formulation of rules and statements of belief, while necessary for this period, have as well a shadow side. The universality and the spontaneity of the initial response are somewhat dulled. With more and more members present, the variety of gifts presents a perennial management problem. How can unity of goal and vision be preserved amidst greater and greater diversity, both in kinds of gifts and in wider geographical dispersion? This drive for preservation of insights has often resulted in the replacement of the original vision by verbal formulations. New members now do not identify with the charism of the founder in an explicit way so much as they tend simply to imitate the examples of community life as they see it lived. Spontaneity of response begins to be replaced by a growing conformity to the verbal formulations.

It is during the expansion period, too, that the first indications occur of a separation between life and service. While there may still be a degree of freedom in the external apostolic thrust, an attempt is made to base the necessary union in a greater conformity to internal structures. Finding that one or two forms of service are especially needed and hence affirmed by society, the community may begin to approve only certain gifts as compatible with what gradually comes to be called the "spirit of the institute." The development is quite subtle, but it provides an efficiency of style and method which produce "success"—and leads directly to the stabilization period.

As the group achieves stabilization, the filter for sorting out the acceptable charisms becomes almost foolproof, and only certain ones are confirmed and approved. This narrowed selectivity operates both internally in its life and externally in its mission. A rather clear example of this is found in the Church itself, which effectively reduced charisms from the rich variety found in the New Testament to only a few gifts which were tied exclusively to a few specific ministries. Even religious life as a charism in the Church was so effectively tied to the juridical institution that it almost completely lost its prophetic character.

Another painfully experienced example of the petrifaction of the stabilization period can be seen in the way offices of leadership came to be assigned. An effort to discern charisms of leadership, of administration, was hardly obvious. In fact, the common understanding seemed to be a complete reversal of such discernment: first the person was elected or appointed, then it was assumed that God would supply the necessary grace! The formation of candidates during the stabilization period provides another example. Seldom was it discerned whether or not the initiate had received the charism of religious life, or of the particular institute. Rather, practically any good Christian man or woman of sound mind and body, and a modicum of good will, was looked on as a worthy candidate.[12]

In an earlier chapter, the transition period was characterized by breakdown and crisis. It is a time of great stress and anxiety. While there is a palpable sense of a new reality, there is an equally palpable lack of adequate words with which to communicate it. The conditioning of long experience makes the warmth and security of rightness, of order, of fixity all too attractive still. While there is an eagerness to return to the primitive spirit, to the pristine vigor of pioneer days, it is still difficult to see just how to slip the knife between calcified accretions and the living nerves, tissue, and bone of vital organisms.[13]

It is important during a transition to see that what is dying

---

[12] Adrian van Kaam, C.S.Sp., has suggested the difficulty in establishing a special spirituality in a congregation because of the admission, during the stabilization period, of much younger candidates whose self-awareness is limited and prevents their "tuning in" in a genuine way with the spirit of the founder (*In Search of a Spiritual Identity* (Denville, N.J.: Dimension Books, 1975), pp. 18–22).

[13] "For very long periods of time, a great majority of members of a given society or parts thereof may be identified with the values and norms of a given system, and willing to provide it with the resources it needs; however, other tendencies also develop. Some groups may be greatly opposed to the very premises of the institutionalization of a given system, may share its values and symbols only to a very small extent and may accept these norms

is probably not the spirit of the founder, not religious life as such. What is dying is the multitude of institutionalized expressions which have been substituted over the years for the founding charism. The death of institutions can bring anger, depression, denial, and all the other emotions that have been associated with the experience of death. Christian faith holds, however, that life lies not in the resistance to death but on the other side of it. The time of breakdown can also be a time of new foundation.[14]

Viewing the charism of a congregation not as an interesting antique but as the gift and call of the Spirit that constantly appears in new forms can provide a more positive way of viewing the transition period. Again and again the Holy Spirit breaks through stale encrustations and topples idols in his work of renewing the face of the earth. Religious life, being prophetic in nature, has an essential role to play in restoring to the Church its appearance as a "Church of fresh breakthrough," a Church which is in constant process of reformation, a Church in which the Spirit operates freely and unrestrainedly.[15]

Part 3: Recovery-Discovery of the Congregation's Charism

As has been already noted several times in the course of these chapters, revitalization demands a process of recovering and

---

only as the least among evils and/or binding on them only in a very limited sense. Others may share these values and symbols and accept the norms to a greater degree, but may look on themselves as the more truthful depositories of these same values. They may oppose the concrete levels at which the symbols are institutionalized by the elite in power. . . . Others may develop new interpretations of existing symbols and norms and strive for a change in the very basis of institutional order. Hence, any institutional system is never fully 'homogeneous' in the sense of being fully accepted or accepted to the same degree by those participating in it. Their different orientations to the central symbolic spheres may all become foci of conflict and of potential institutional change" (Weber, p. xliv).

[14] Gerlach and Hine suggest the problem of "focusing on movements or mechanisms of change rather than on the conditions of disorganization which give rise to them" (p. xiv).

[15] K. Rahner, "On the Evangelical Counsels," *Theological Investigations*, vol. 8 (New York: Herder and Herder, 1971), p. 134.

discovering. It is a dialogic process. There is more to considering charism, then, than simple research into the life of the founder and the early history of the order or congregation. It is essential not only to know the times of the founder and his/her response to those times through the exercise of particular gifts, but to know the present times as well and to recognize what gifts the members have which enable a response.

A cursory reading of *Perfectae Caritatis* and *Evangelica Testificatio* reveals a number of words and phrases that ought to enter into a discussion of how a congregation goes about discovering its charisms. These are: "an institute's own proper character and function," "spirit and aims of the founder," "sound traditions," "patrimony of the institute," "charisms of the founders," "evangelical intention of the founder," "example of the founder's sanctity," "charism of religious life as a fruit of the Holy Spirit," and "dynamism proper to each institute." John Futrell[16] has advised that the discovery of the founder's charism must be based on adequate historical research, the goal of which is "to describe as accurately as possible the founder's personal conception of the life and action of the community he founded." He further states that it is the *profound intention* underlying the founder's historically and culturally conditioned expression which must be brought to light, and insists on "the spiritual continuity of charism . . . across the radical discontinuity of its historical and cultural expressions." "The charism of the founder of any religious community is this charism as it is lived now," states Futrell, and points out several distinctions, which, if not defining positively what this historical reality (the charism of the founder who presumably lived in the past) is, at least indicate what its being present now does *not* mean: 1) no historical expression of it, even the founder's, fixes the movement once and for all; 2) it cannot be identified with a particular spiritual vocabulary of the founder's time;

---

[16] J. C. Futrell, "Discovering the Founder's Charism," *The Way*, Supplement 14 (Fall 1971) 65.

3) the founder's ideal of apostolic service cannot be identified with particular works. On the other hand, the purpose in studying the life, works, and words of the founder is to articulate in the language of our own times the *authentic vision* of the founder such that it becomes the ideal and norm for contemporary spiritual renewal and adaptation. Nevertheless, this authentic vision cannot be fixed in abstract, verbal definitions (even contemporary ones) but must be brought to life in actual living members of the congregation. This is done by bringing "to the level of conscious awareness the charismatic call which they share and which they are experiencing and living."

The delineation-by-negation approach employed by Futrell, however, leaves the distinct impression that one has continued to "peel the onion" to the point that it becomes extremely difficult to get hold of the *profound intention* of the founder, since one is not supposed to identify it with his/her words, spirituality, or forms of apostolic service. What, then, is this reality which present members are now supposed to share, dialogue with, and articulate in contemporary language? Some questions can be posed which may point the way to developing some images or models which may reduce the elusiveness and the possibly unsatisfying result of the process of discovering the founder's charism.

1. *Does every particular congregation have a founder who can be said to have a specific charism?* It appears from a study of the history of religious life that certain founders can be viewed as truly prophetic as they struck out on a path of religious life that was previously uncharted. At some point during their lives, if not in the earliest days of foundation, some of these prophetic men and women likewise were able to explicate not only an understanding of their mission, but also the means and methods whereby the vision was to be realized. Ignatius Loyola and William Joseph Chaminade come immediately to mind. Others, just as truly prophetic and pioneering, presented a strong sense of direction but were not quite so precise as to method and means. But there are numerous congregations of religious, most often women, who trace their

founding to what appears to be no more than the functional decision of a bishop who needed teachers for his school or nurses for a Catholic health-care facility in his diocese. Frequently the choice of a rule seemed to be simply the adoption of some form of a previously existing rule already approved by the Church.

Congregations founded by men or women who were not only visionary but also gifted with organizational foresight usually have little problem in reappropriating the vision and often enough even the means and method of the founder. In the case of the congregations whose founding was more functionary than visionary, there would appear to be several options. The group may identify more clearly for itself the spiritual tradition of the adopted rule to determine if some eclectic application of the rule in their case has actually deprived them of balancing insights provided by the original creator of the rule. Another approach, not different from what every congregation must do but more essential for these, would be to analyze the actual history of the congregation in order to determine what the predominant values were that consistently undergirded the life decisions of the congregation as it moved through history. This process might lead to a reaffirmation of the congregation's self-image such that it would provide a real thrust for revitalization. An even more challenging possibility is for the group to ask itself whether or not, if they were not in existence, they ought to come into existence in order to respond to a clear call sounding from the signs of the times. This could provide the exciting possibility of a really new foundation.

2. *Is there a difference between the founder's charism and the spirit of the founder?* If charisms are gifts given for the sake of service, it seems clear that one of the specific charisms of the founder was to found a new approach to fulfilling the general command of the gospel. The other gifts of the founder—personality, talents for leadership and organization, imagination, etc.—provide what might be considered a certain style or spirit to the new institute. Both the charism to found and the spirit or style belong to the founder in a unique way that

is different from, even though it is shared with, what we might call the "founding community."

3. *What is the relationship, then, between the founder and the founding community, that is, to that small group which understood, identified with, and supported the implementation of the founder's vision?* Obviously, without the founding community which assured the perdurance of the founder's vision there would be nothing to be rediscovered in our own time. But, even more importantly, the interrelationship between the founder and each of the original members, as well as between the founder and the founding community as a whole, must be explored. A certain hermeneutical approach in studying this interrelationship might reveal, for example, that certain elements considered essential or basic by the founder may not have been implemented because of certain limitations in the original group. Such limitations may have been in the area of particular skills, economic lack, or simply in resistance from certain members. Viewed from a certain historical distance, however, these basic elements can be rediscovered and now implemented, the previous limitations no longer binding.[17]

The existence of the founding community, with its particular complex of personal charisms which interacted with those of the founding person, seems to indicate that whatever the "community charism" is it most certainly has a mosaic-like quality and a richness of scope. Most histories of religious orders do not permit a description of the community's charism as being limiting in the sense of being monolithic. Granted, this mosaic is special and unique in that it is *this* particular interrelationship of gifts placed at the service of *this* particular vision of the gospel, and is thus different from

---

[17] The hermeneutic approach in studying sacred scripture has proven its immense usefulness. See Thomas B. Ommen, "The Hermeneutic of Dogma," *Theological Studies* 35 (1974) 605–31, where the extension of this approach to the treatment of dogmatic statements is surveyed. There is no reason to think that the hermeneutic principle ought not to be applied to the history and documents of a given congregation.

other entities in which similar gifts may be found but not in precisely the same relationship. But it is a rich complex of gifts and not a dismal repetition of the same gifts in each member. The members, though identifying with the founder, are not simple carbon copies!

Part 4: The Recovery-Discovery Process and Foundational Texts

The most concrete way of coming to know the mind of the founder is by making use of foundational texts. A successful dialogue with these texts will depend on establishing and making accessible the whole corpus of the writings of the founder, understanding the historical circumstances of the writings, and appreciating the language and symbols that are used.

Initially, a critical study must be made of the founding texts in order to establish which were the founder's own, and which were the work of associates. These texts will appear in a variety of literary forms. None should be neglected, but the value of each should be distinguished. For example, letters of the founder are important in a different way from the legal decrees that formed the canonical basis for the foundation of the community. Community chronicles are much different from the symbolic prose that might have been employed in spiritual conferences and instructions that have been passed down in written form. Retreat notes and journals might reveal more of the private devotion and piety of the founder, while letters to others might reveal more of his or her intentions for the foundation, and of the circumstances and persons which influenced it. Each of these forms can transmit insights about the founding charism. The task of critical interpretation of texts is complex and demanding. Many religious communities, however, have members who possess the skills necessary for such basic investigation.

Establishing the historical situation in which the founder wrote is the second essential stage of interpretation of texts. Certain emphases, for example, in spirituality or lifestyle might not seem excessive when they are understood as being necessary to restore a balance lost at a particular time in history. The historical situation must obviously be determined with the help of other documents outside the foundational texts in order to determine which were the defects, merits, or excesses of the period which the founder addressed. To apply literally the words of the founder when such a situation no longer prevails would do great disservice to the founding vision and spirit.

An appreciation of the language and symbols used by the founder follows from the first two tasks of interpretation. In their original context, foundational writings were frequently both immediate and personal. Intended for specific circumstances, the texts may allude to matters of knowledge, experience, or expectations common to the founder and his or her contemporaries. In a later period, however, these foundational texts can have a meaning which transcends their original use. Although they are literary artifacts, such texts do not remain anchored in their original historical situation but are able to take on new meanings in new historical settings. As mentioned in an earlier chapter, the hermeneutical methodology applied so productively to sacred scripture must be used as well in drawing out the symbolic meaning of the founder's writings, avoiding their mere literal interpretation.

Determining the texts and their historical context and appreciating their literary forms and symbols provide the basis for a productive dialogue with the founder and the founding community. A community, however, must bring important contemporary questions to the texts of its foundations and attempt to find there not so much the answers to present questions as the resources for a meaningful interpretation of its contemporary situation. In such a dialogue it is important for the community to recognize the effects of time and culture, not only in the foundation texts, but in its own principles and reflections. Not only must it pose contemporary questions to the founder, but the community must permit the founder, through the texts, to question its own understanding of life and of life situations.

Part 5: Response to the Charism and a New Self-Image

What remains is to suggest some possible images or models which might serve not only to free a congregation to engage wholeheartedly in recovering and reappropriating its charism, but will also produce a more concrete and satisfying result.

In his "Observations on the Factor of the Charismatic in the Church," Karl Rahner argues convincingly for the nature of the Church as an "open system," over which God presides as Lord. He distinguishes a "closed system" as "a complex of realities of various kinds which, despite their variations, are related to one another and contribute towards a common task, . . . defined and directed from a point within the system itself." An "open system," on the other hand, is

> . . . such that the definitive condition in which it actually stands and should stand neither can nor should be defined in any adequate sense in terms of any one point immanent within the system itself. On the contrary, its definitive state can only be defined in terms of a point outside the system, i.e. in terms of the dominion of God, so that to do justice to the state in which the system exists at any given stage, we must say that its operations are charismatic rather than institutional in character. (p. 89)

What can be said about a healthy universal structure of the Church ought to be applicable as well to each smaller unit within it, including the religious community. If the religious community is to be a shining example of the Church operating at its optimum level, the "open system" would seem to offer the best operating model. The model, providing for a complex of various but related realities, contributing toward a common task and defined in terms of a point outside the system, corresponds to the demand for a revitalized community that is in tune with the spirit of the gospel, the charism of the founder, and the signs of the times. The model connotes interdependence in the life and service of the congregation. Its definition from a point outside itself, "the dominion of God," would seem to assure a continuing response to an ever-renewed call demanding an ongoing process of transformation of persons and revision of structures.[18] The limitations of its "realities"—a particular history, a shared vision, a given group of persons—would suffice to root it firmly without burying it in its past.

Another useful model might be derived from the Hebrew concept of the corporate personality. Philip Kaufman has shown that while this concept is not found as such in the Bible, it does express "the Hebrew ideas of anthropology and psychology which underlie conceptions of the relationship of the community and the individual in both Old and New Testaments."[19] This concept provides a useful analogy for the continuity of relationship between the founder and the present-day community. "The community is one because it has a common character and a common history going back to a common ancestor," and "the relation of the leader or ancestor to the community is to be seen in the nature of blessing." The founder lived on in the children, the bearer of his name, and their name was character-bearing. Our concept of *esprit de corps* pales by comparison with a sense that "the whole group, including its past, present and future members, might function as a single individual through any one of those members conceived as representative of it." The concept does not deal with fiction or mere poetic personification, but refers to a real entity. If, as is often said, the bonds of faith are stronger than bonds of blood, then could not the corporate personality be a most effective image of the religious com-

---

[18] This sense of being defined by a point outside itself serves to prevent members from merely basking in a mythic reality of call with no sense of demand on one's life. Sr. Marie Augusta Neal, S.N.D.de N., contributed this insight in a lecture dealing with the results of the 1967 National Sisters' Survey. "If the Sisters agreed on anything, it was on the fact that they were called. Called to what? 'To follow Jesus' would be the customary response." "But then," says Sr. Marie Augusta, "the question is 'Jesus, where are you going?' The one place we are sure Jesus is, is with his people" (Lecture to Sisters of Charity of Seton Hill, 20 June 1976).

[19] Philip Kaufman, "The One and the Many: Corporate Personality," *Worship* 42 (November 1968) 546–55. All the quotations here are from this article.

munity, supplying, as does the previously suggested model, the emphasis on interdependence and mutuality. The unity possible amidst a diversity of charisms is more readily understandable by reference to the concept of the corporate personality.

Corporateness more adequately describes what it is that distinguishes the religious institute whose members live in common than the word *community*. This is suggested not simply to multiply concepts nor yet to accent differences. It does seem, however, that meanings of "community" from sociological, psychological, and religious contexts have become common parlance in our society, such that the word is not too useful any longer to describe satisfactorily what exactly constitutes the religious "community," since its members frequently find themselves valid members of other genuine "communities." What is suggested here is to use the word "corporate" to describe that entity which results when individuals commit their lives to one another, to the Church, and to God, and thus to distinguish it from commitment merely to a common project or endeavor of a more temporary sort. Community comes from the Latin words *cum* and *munire* and literally means "to build together." Thus the corporate entity when it engages in transforming reality (to use the words of Freire) is also a community. But it is more than that.

A final and more poetic metaphor useful for understanding the interrelatedness of the past, present, and future of the corporate entity is that of the tree. Through the founding person's transformation in Christ and his or her compelling image of the future, the community was planted so that it was firmly rooted in Christ. The tree has many branches, and at the end of the branches are leaves, blossoms, fruit. These latter grow, develop, die, and drop off. If their source, the tree, is rooted firmly and vitally, however, there will be still more new leaves, new blossoms, new fruit, so long as the roots continue to be cultivated. It is at the level of the leaves, blossoms, and fruit that we are called upon to be creative, innovative, free. Occasionally a branch may even be pruned without grief. Most important, illness or blight on the leaves, the blossoms, or the fruit can be traced to many causes—disease, drought, climate. And sometimes they are signs of a tree that is diseased or dead at its roots.

The task of revitalization is centered around the question of a community's rootedness in Christ and in the spirit of the founder. Contemporary adaptations in forms of service and lifestyle can only be productive to the extent that this radical transformation is an ongoing process. Everything the community is and does will then be organically related, and its life will be stable while remaining flexible and free.

What has been suggested in this chapter are simply some areas for exploration in which some preliminary work has been done. Christian theologians, sociologists, and philosophers need to continue to explore the diverse aspects of the nature of charism. When this is accomplished, the self-understanding not only of religious communities but of the Church itself will be greatly enhanced.

Further Reading

Besides works already cited in footnotes or noted at the end of Chapter Five, readers may care to refer to the following books and articles for additional reading on the various subjects touched in the chapters of this book.

The abbreviation *RFR* stands for *Review for Religious*.

1. History of Religious Life (General)

Bausch, William J. *Pilgrim Church: A Popular History of Catholic Christianity*. Notre Dame, Ind.: Fides, 1973. Paperback edition: 1978.

Bokenkotter, Thomas. *A Concise History of the Catholic Church*. Garden City, N.Y.: Doubleday, 1977.

Cain, James R. "Cloister and the Apostolate of Religious Women." *RFR* 27 (March, May, July, September 1968) 243–80, 427–48, 652–71, 916–37, and 28 (January 1969) 101–21.

Engels, Odilio. "Religious Orders," in *Sacramentum Mundi*, vol. 5 (New York: Herder and Herder, 1970), pp. 298–315.

Gannon, Thomas M., S. J., and Traub, George W., S.J. *The Desert and the City*. London: Macmillan, 1969.

Hostie, Raymond, S.J. *Vie et mort des ordres religieux*. Paris: Desclée de Brouwer, 1972. An English translation of this work is being prepared for publication by CARA (Center for Applied Research in the Apostolate) in Washington.

Knowles, David, O.S.B. *Christian Monasticism*. New York: McGraw-Hill, 1969.

Mohler, James A., S.J. *The Heresy of Monasticism.* New York: Alba House, 1971.

Van Allen, Roger. "Religious Life and Christian Vocation." *Cross Currents* 22 (1972) 171–82.

Vicaire, M. H., O.P. *The Apostolic Life.* Chicago: Priory Press, 1966.

2. History of Religious Life (*Particular Traditions*)

Bangert, William V., S.J. *A History of the Society of Jesus.* St. Louis, Mo.: Institute of Jesuit Sources, 1972.

Brooke, Rosalind B. *The Coming of the Friars.* New York: Barnes & Noble, 1975.

Doyle, Eric, O.F.M. "Seven-hundred-and-fifty Years Later: Reflections on the Franciscan Charism." *RFR* 36 (January 1977) 12–35.

Habig, Marion A., ed. *St. Francis of Assisi: Omnibus of Sources.* Chicago: Franciscan Herald Press, 1973.

Hilpisch, Stephanus, O.S.B. *Benedictinism through Changing Centuries.* Collegeville, Minn.: St. John's Abbey Press, 1958.

———. *History of Benedictine Nuns.* Collegeville, Minn.: St. John's Abbey Press, 1958.

Hinnebusch, William A., O.P. *The Dominicans: A Short History.* New York: Alba House, 1975.

———. *The History of the Dominican Order,* 2 vols. New York: Alba House, 1966–73.

———. "How the Dominican Order Faced Its Crises." *RFR* 32 (November 1973) 1307–21.

Isabell, Damien, O.F.M. *Workbook for Franciscan Studies: Companion Guide to the Omnibus of Sources.* Chicago: Franciscan Herald Press, 1975.

Ledochowska, Teresa, O.S.U. *Angela Merici and the Company of St. Ursula,* 2 vols. Rome: Ancora, 1969.

Pastor, Bartholomew, T.O.R. "The 'State of Penance' and the Beginnings of the Order of the Brothers and Sisters of Penance." *Analecta Tertii Ordinis Regularsi Sancti Francisci* 13 (1974) 35–72.

3. *Founders, Foundresses and Founding Charisms*

Brockman, Norbert, S.M. "Directed Prayer and the Founding Charism." *RFR* 33 (March 1974) 257–64.

Futrell, John Carroll, S.J. "Discovering the Founder's Charism." *The Way* Supplement 14 (Fall 1971) 62–70.

————. "Some Reflections on the Religious Life." *RFR* 28 (September 1969) 705–18.

George, Francis E., O.M.I. "Founding 'Founderology': Charism and Hermeneutics." *RFR* 36 (January 1977) 40–48.

Ledochowska, Teresa, O.S.U. *In Search of the Charism of the Institute.* Rome: Ursulines of the Roman Union, 1976.

Lozano, Juan Manuel, C.M.F. "Founder and Community: Inspiration and Charism." *RFR* 37 (March 1978) 214–36.

McCarty, Shaun, S.T. "Religious Roots: Knowing and Owning Our Story," *RFR* 37 (January 1978) 117–22.

————. "Touching Each Other at the Roots: A Reflection on the Charism of the Founder." *RFR* 31 (March 1972) 202–205.

Molinari, Paul, S.J. "Religious Renewal and the Founder's Spirit." *RFR* 27 (September 1968) 796–806.

Whitley, Cuthbert Michael, O.S.B. "Revitalizing Religious Life: Some Operations on the Phenomenon of Charisma." *RFR* 36 (January 1977) 70–77.

4. *Religious Life and the Future*

Brockman, Norbert, S.M. "Burnout in Superiors." *RFR* 37 (November 1978) 809–16.

Fitz, Raymond, S.M., and Cada, Lawrence, S.M. "The Recovery of Religious Life." *RFR* 34 (September 1975) 690–718.

Hocking, William Ernest. *The Coming World Civilization.* London: George Allen and Unwin, 1958.

Malo, Jean, S.S.S., ed. *Religious Life: Tomorrow.* Donum Dei Series no. 24. Ottawa: Canadian Religious Conference, 1978. Proceedings of the Third Interamerican Meeting of Religious held in Montreal in November 1977.

Toolan, David S., S.J. "Pilgrims in a Strange World." *Commonweal* 105 (June 16, 1978) 399–404.

Thompson, William Irwin. *Evil and World Order*. New York: Harper & Row, 1976.

5. *Spirituality and Theology of Religious Life*

Balthasar, Hans Urs von. "A Theology of the Evangelical Counsels." *Cross Currents* 16 (1966) 213–36, 325–39.

Matura, Thadée, O.F.M. *The Crisis of Religious Life*. Chicago: Franciscan Herald Press, 1973.

Murphy-O'Connor, Jerome, O.P. *What is Religious Life?* Wilmington, Del.: Michael Glazier, 1977.

O'Meara, Thomas F., O.P. *Holiness and Radicalism in Religious Life*. New York: Herder and Herder, 1970.

Rahner, Karl, S.J. "On the Evangelical Counsels," in *Theological Investigations,* vol. 8 (New York: Herder and Herder, 1971), pp. 133–67. Another translation of this article appears under the title "The Theology of Religious Life," in *Religious Orders in the Modern World* by Gerard Huyghe et al. (Westminster, Md.: Newman Press, 1966), pp. 41–75. The article is summarized in *Theology Digest* 14 (1966) 224–27.

———. "Reflections on a Theology of Renunciation," in *Theological Investigations,* vol. 3 (Baltimore: Helicon Press, 1967), pp. 47–57.

Seasoltz, Kevin, O.S.B. *Consider Your Call*. London: S.P.C.K., 1978.

Tillard, J. M. R., O.P. *A Gospel Path: The Religious Life*. Brussels: Lumen Vitae Press, 1975.

6. *Charisms, Hermeneutics, Process and Grace*

Gadamer, Hans-Georg. *Truth and Method*. New York: Seabury Press, 1975.

Gelpi, Donald, S.J. *Charism and Sacrament: A Theology of Christian Conversion*. New York: Paulist Press, 1976.

———. *Experiencing God: A Theology of Human Experience*. New York: Paulist Press, 1978.

Lee, Bernard, S.M. *The Becoming of the Church: A Process*

Theology of the Structures of Christian Experience. New York: Paulist Press, 1974.

Ommen, Thomas B. "The Hermeneutic of Dogma." *Theological Studies* 35 (December 1974) 605–31.

Palmer, Richard E. *Hermeneutics.* Evanston, Ill.: Northwestern University Press, 1969.

Rahner, Karl, S.J. "Charism," in *Encyclopedia of Theology: The Concise "Sacramentum Mundi"* (New York: Seabury Press, 1975), pp. 184–86.

———. *The Dynamic Element in the Church.* New York: Herder and Herder, 1964.

———. "Observations on the Factor of the Charismatic in the Church," in *Theological Investigations,* vol. 12 (New York: Seabury Press, 1974), pp. 81–97.

Ricoeur, Paul. "The Hermeneutical Function of Distanciation." *Philosophy Today* 17 (1973) 129–41.

———. "Philosophical Hermeneutics and Theological Hermeneutics." *Sciences Religieuses/Studies in Religion* 5 (1975) 14–33.

———. "The Task of Hermeneutics." *Philosophy Today* 17 (1973) 112–28.

Tracy, David. *Blessed Rage for Order: The New Pluralism in Theology.* New York: Seabury Press, 1975.

7. Social Evolution and Organizational Change

Berger, Peter L., and Luckmann, Thomas. *The Social Construction of Reality: A Treatise in the Sociology of Knowledge.* Garden City, N.Y.: Anchor Books, 1967.

Gerlach, Luther P., and Hine, Virginia H. *People, Power, Change: Movements of Social Transformation.* Indianapolis, Ind.: Bobbs-Merrill, 1970.

Heilbroner, Robert L. *An Inquiry into the Human Prospect.* New York: W. W. Norton, 1974.

Kuhn, Thomas S. *The Structure of Scientific Revolutions,* 2d ed. Chicago: University of Chicago Press, 1970.

Turner, Victor. *Dramas, Fields, and Metaphors: Symbolic Action in Human Society.* Ithaca, N.Y.: Cornell University Press, 1974.

Authors

All five authors were part of the Marianist Training Network, and since 1974 have designed and conducted numerous workshops and renewal programs for men and women religious.

Lawrence Cada, S.M., Ph.D., is Marianist Formation Coordinator for Kenya, where he also teaches mathematics and philosophy at the Nairobi Extension of the University of Dayton. He has facilitated workshops in North America and East Africa on founding charisms and the history and renewal of religious life. Brother Cada has served as an advisor to several Marianist lay communities. He has held a number of formation positions in his province of the Society of Mary, and is involved in various programs studying Marianist history and the Marianist charism. Formerly he taught mathematics and philosophy at Western Michigan University, Cleveland State University, and the University of Dayton, and was chair of the Science and Mathematics Department at Borromeo College of Ohio in Wickliffe.

Raymond L. Fitz, S.M., Ph.D., has been President of the University of Dayton since 1979. Brother Fitz held appointments as Professor of Engineering Management and Electrical Engineering in addition to directing the Center for Christian Renewal at the University of Dayton. He has directed projects in fields such as planning, organization development, and management and design of large-scale systems.

Gertrude Foley, S.C., D.Min., is a member of the Sisters of Charity of Seton Hill, Greensburg, Pennsylvania. In addition to extensive experience in education and in community administration, she has worked with numerous religious congregations in the United States, Canada, and Australia in programs of renewal and planning. Her chief interests lie in the fields of historical theology, futures studies, and pastoral ministry.

Thomas F. Giardino, S.M., M.A., is presently consultant for Small Christian Communities for the Diocese of Kalamazoo, Michigan. Brother Giardino served for many years as executive editor of the Marianist Resources Commission, an international publication program of documentation for the Society of Mary. He is experienced in retreat work, consultancies, and renewal programs in the United States, East Africa, and Australia.

Carol Lichtenberg, S.N.D.deN., M.Ed., is director of community life for the Ohio province of the Sisters of Notre Dame of Namur in Cincinnati, Ohio. She is active in the application of planning approaches to various institutional settings. She also serves on the provincial team and is a member of the Leadership Conference of Women Religious.

INDEX